THE
staub
COOKBOOK

THE
staub
COOKBOOK

MODERN RECIPES FOR CLASSIC CAST IRON

Staub

with **Amanda Frederickson**

Photography by **Colin Price**

TEN SPEED PRESS
California | New York

CONTENTS

INTRODUCTION

Welcome. We're so glad you could join us. We wrote this book with your dinner table and you in mind. You, the beginner who has always wanted to try cooking with cast iron. You, the seasoned chef who shares our love for this remarkable material. You, the Staub owner who wants inspiration for Sunday suppers. We've poured our expertise into these pages to help you make the most out of your cast-iron cookware.

Staub cast iron isn't just gourmet kitchenware. It inspires people to cook, and to cook better, to try new recipes, and to share meals with loved ones. Staub brings people together in the kitchen, online, around the table for a delicious meal, and, now, in these pages.

When we set out to compile our first-ever cookbook, we knew we wanted it to be a community affair. Our cookware is beloved by notable chefs from around the world, as well as countless home cooks. The recipes would need to resonate with all of them. So we turned to a cook we've long admired for elevating everyday affairs: Amanda Frederickson. As it turned out, she loves Staub as much as we love her cooking.

From there, we checked in with friends: chefs, influencers, and other professionals who believe in our cookware as much as we do. Many responded in minutes. They contributed recipes that are a mix of classics and inventive spins. Then we added a few traditional French dishes, a nod to the company's roots in France, and some weeknight and weekend morning dishes. The goal was to compile approachable and inviting recipes that pique the palates of all home chefs—from amateur to gourmet.

You'll notice that there is not a "how-to" section or a glossary of ingredients. We aim to inspire by doing: cook a recipe and you'll learn techniques or maybe even a new flavor combination, while getting a delicious dinner, breakfast, or dessert on the table. We'll give you the tools to make the most out of our cookware every time. The braised chicken on page 142 is exceptional as it is, but the second time you give it a go you might want to riff—lemons and capers? Citrus and thyme? Be our guest.

Ever since the day Francis Staub brought his first cocottes to a few local stores in Alsace, France, all of our cookware has been made from enameled cast iron. Sturdy but not unwieldy, the heft of a Staub fry pan alone is enough to instill confidence in any cook, not to mention the guarantee of even heat and a good sear.

Unlike traditional cast-iron cookware, Staub is remarkably easy to care for—it can be washed with soap and doesn't need to be seasoned. The exteriors have a colorful sheen, in hues and silhouettes crafted to feel classic for eternity because they *will* actually last that long—it's one of the things that makes Staub so revered. Which is perhaps why we see our cocottes everywhere, set proudly on your stoves even when you're not cooking with them. We spot them on restaurant tables, as much a part of the decor as the actual decor, and out in the open in chefs' carefully considered restaurant kitchens. They command pride of place wherever they go.

We've subtitled this compilation *Modern Recipes for Classic Cast Iron* to reflect the way so many of us cook today. We want quick and flavorful weeknight dinners, but we might invest a little more time and effort on weekends or when we're entertaining. So you'll find recipes for make-ahead breakfasts and slow-rise breads, twenty-minute dinners and long-simmered specialties. You can start small or go big right off the bat—we simply invite you to celebrate the pleasures of cooking.

Bon appétit!

THE STAUB COCOTTE
A ONE-POT WONDER

Francis Staub created the first Staub cocotte in 1974, inspired by the late, legendary French chef Paul Bocuse. An instant hit, his "perfect pot" is still the darling of top chefs worldwide. In vibrant colors, this premium French-made enameled cast-iron cocotte is a modern heirloom that is as appealing to the palate as it is to the eye.

Oven-safe knobs (to 500°F) are nickel-plated stainless steel or brass. These metals are specially chosen because they withstand high temperatures without tarnishing.

Staub's signature interior is a quartz-studded black matte enamel that creates the ideal surface for browning, searing, and caramelizing foods. And the best part is, it doesn't need to be seasoned, making cleaning fast and easy.

Staub cocottes are designed with a self-basting lid system (see image, right). The lid's spikes, flatness, weight, and tight fit create a perfect environment for steam to rise, condense, and evenly drip back onto the food for more tenderness and flavor.

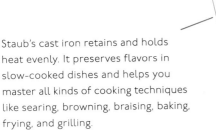

Our products are extremely durable and resistant to scratches, chips, and stains.

Staub's cast iron retains and holds heat evenly. It preserves flavors in slow-cooked dishes and helps you master all kinds of cooking techniques like searing, browning, braising, baking, frying, and grilling.

Francis Staub pioneered our stunning *majolique* color technique. It creates long-lasting, eye-catching enamel shades with color highs and lows in each unique piece.

The smooth enamel base is suitable for all cooktops, including induction.

WHAT IS A COCOTTE?

co·cotte
/kôˈkôt/
noun

1. A traditional French oven.

2. A covered cast-iron pot in which food can be heated and served.

3. A must-have for braises, stews, and one-pot dishes.

USE AND CARE

TOOLS OF THE TRADE

- Don't worry if you don't have the specific Staub piece listed in the recipe. Our suggested pans are guides, not absolutes. So if you don't have an oval baker, go ahead and use a rectangular baker or a similarly sized fry pan. Or swap a petite French oven for a sauce pan.

- For reference, a medium fry pan is 10 inches, a medium cocotte holds 4 or 5½ quarts, and our petite French oven holds 1½ quarts.

CARING FOR YOUR STAUB

- Though dishwasher safe, washing by hand is recommended. Your Staub is easy to clean with everyday dish soap.

- For stuck-on grease, clean the interior and exterior with a non-abrasive cleaner and a soft brush or sponge. Heating your pan on the stove with soapy warm water in it also helps loosen up cooked-on bits.

- Avoid abrasive metal sponges.

- We recommend using silicone or wooden tools to prevent the interior enamel from scratching.

- Always leave a hot pan to cool down before cleaning to avoid thermal shock.

- Never place your Staub in the microwave.

GETTING TO KNOW YOUR STAUB

- Unlike traditional cast iron, our black matte enamel interior is safe for storing food. Make a tomato sauce and refrigerate it in the same pan. The sauce will taste great plus the pot will be a cinch to clean.

- Letting your food stick to your Staub is a good thing. Once you place your protein inside, it will initially stick and that's okay. Your food will let you know when it's ready to be flipped, since it will easily release once it is properly seared.

- Staub is designed with storage in mind. Simply invert the cocotte lids for easy stacking or nest our bakers.

- For perfect oven basting, try putting ice cubes on the lid. The cooler temperature will create additional condensation for automatic basting.

- You can use your cocotte lid as a press—bring on the paninis and brick chicken.

- Cocottes can go camping too. Put your cocotte in a fire pit with coals on the lid. Heat will come from below and above, creating a smoke-fired oven.

- Staub can go straight onto an outdoor grill. If your grill is dirty, be warned that grease can get onto your cookware.

SERVE UP YOUR STAUB

- Your Staub doubles as a stylish serving dish, going from oven to table effortlessly.

- Enameled cast iron keeps cold dishes cool and hot food hot. Try freezing ice cream in a loaf pan, or serve a cold side dish or salad in a chilled roasting pan. Gravy stays warm—and looks quite chic—when served in our tea kettle.

- 1 quart = 1 serving size. So dinner for 4 to 6 is best made in our 5.5-quart cocotte—our best-selling size.

roasters

petite french oven

coq au vin

fry pans

cocottes

THE HISTORY OF STAUB
WHERE IT ALL BEGAN

Rewind almost half a century. Francis Staub—the grandson of a cookware salesman—started his business by purchasing an old artillery factory in the homeland of one-pot cooking: Alsace, France. Although cast-iron cookware had already been in use for hundreds of years, it was cumbersome to care for and had an industrial appearance. Francis Staub had a solution: by adding modern enameling to the cocotte, the region's celebrated covered casserole, cast iron was elevated to an exquisite, easy-to-clean material. Voilà, the perfect pot was born.

Our signature textured black matte enamel interior is what sets us apart. This innovative surface boasts perfect browning and a stellar sear for the most flavorful dishes. And it becomes better with age—as cooking fats penetrate the pores of the matte enamel, it creates a naturally smooth surface. Along with its exceptional durability, the black matte enamel performs like a pro when tested in a demanding restaurant environment—where a week of use rivals a year in a home kitchen.

Francis Staub collaborated with the world's best chefs to create premium cookware that is endlessly functional in the kitchen and beautifully transitions to the table. As the acclaimed chef Paul Bocuse puts it, "French cuisine would not be what it is today without all these dishes that cook slowly in a cocotte. Staub cocottes are really well-designed, high-performance products."

Throughout the years, Staub products have multiplied. What began as a top-of-the-line, enameled cast-iron cocotte has evolved into a whole collection of kitchenware with the latest cooking technologies: a smooth, induction-friendly base now gleams on every pot, so that they can be used on any cooktops. Our lids are designed with either chistera curves or self-basting spikes on the inside (see image page xi), which create continuous condensation for the most succulent braises, flavorful stews, and tender grains.

With almost fifty years in the industry, we've learned an enormous amount, adapting our products without disrupting the classic look and feel our customers love.

THE MAKING OF STAUB
HOW THE MAGIC HAPPENS

Today, Staub cast-iron cookware is fabricated in our foundry just outside of Merville, a small village surrounded by charming canals in northern France. Walking through the foundry's doors you can't help but spot the two blazing thirty-foot-tall furnaces as a whole ton of sparking and shimmering molten cast iron will shuttle right past you in a forklift.

Many of Staub's employees live in the surrounding towns, with some second-generation workers at the foundry: from scientists who test our new enamel color recipes to ensure they can scale up to a batch of thousands, to a superman who cleans out those towering furnaces every day (his dad held the position before him). Apparently, Staub runs in the family.

As with any heirloom-quality object made in high volume, our process relies on both human and machine. A single Staub cocotte is handled by more than twenty people over the course of its production. Once fresh from the kiln, a few pots from every few thousand are singled out, tested, and recycled to make sure the batch is of exceptional quality (without a doubt, every single one must be).

The whole process takes place in this foundry, using some of the same systems Francis Staub put in place those many years ago. It all starts with a pile of raw materials. Nearly a ton of pig iron, scrap metal, fuel, and limestone is layered into one of the two-story-high furnaces (called *cupolas*), which are then heated to a rip-roaring 2550°F.

Once molten, the mixture is ladled into sand molds, which produce cookware shapes just three to four millimeters thick (an eventual layer of enameled glass spread over the exterior is what bulks them up). Hitting the air, they harden in just twenty seconds. We then send them down a jittering conveyor belt where workers help chip off extra bits of sand mold from the handles and lids. From there, it's a matter of finessing: rough patches are shot-blasted off the sides or even ground away by hand for more intricate shapes like the tomato and pumpkin pots, until they're smooth and refined around every turn.

Then enameling is applied to each cocotte. Our *majolique* finishes get extra coats, resulting in that watery sheen. The material is a combination of crushed glass, pigment, and clay mixed up with a bit of water that's sprayed onto the pots as they spin and twirl gracefully along the line.

It's not all about getting a pristinely smooth surface. Two different kinds of glass, with two different melting points, are used to make the insides of each pot coarse and matte—just one of them melts in the 1470°F kiln while the other stays solid. Once cooled, they are rigorously quality tested for acid resistance (so there's no problem cooking tomato soup), impact resistance (everybody drops a pot now and again), and thermal shock resistance (but it's not a good idea to put any hot pot under cold water).

Every piece of Staub cookware that hits retail shelves throughout the world is made in this foundry—and we take just as much pride in the process as the result. A cook thinks the same way, selecting time-tested recipes, choosing high-quality ingredients, and using first-rate cookware for delicious results. So go on: bookmark a few pages. Pick up some groceries. It's time to put your Staub to work.

BREAKFAST & BRUNCH

Chocolate Babka Morning Buns 4

Buckwheat Crepes with Egg,
Ham, and Cheese 8

Cinnamon Apple Puffed Pancake 11

Spicy Tofu and
Vegetable Scramble 12

Mixed-Berry Baked Oatmeal 13

Kale Shakshuka with Garlic,
Feta, and Lemon 14

Grilled French Toast and Peaches
with Whipped Cream 17

Savory Dutch Baby with Prosciutto,
Fontina, and Fried Eggs 18

Peanut Butter, Chocolate Chip,
and Coconut Granola Bars 19

Asparagus, Chanterelle, and
Chèvre Frittata with Chervil 20

Vanilla Bean Old-Fashioned
Doughnuts 23

CHOCOLATE BABKA MORNING BUNS

FROM MICHELLE LOPEZ OF *HUMMINGBIRD HIGH*

MAKES 7 TO 9 BUNS

BUTTERMILK DOUGH

3½ cups all-purpose flour, plus more if needed

3 tablespoons granulated sugar

1 tablespoon instant yeast

½ teaspoon baking soda

1 teaspoon kosher salt

1 cup buttermilk, warmed to 110°F, plus more if needed

1 large egg

¼ cup vegetable oil

CHOCOLATE FILLING

8 ounces dark chocolate, chopped

¼ cup unsalted butter, at room temperature

¼ cup packed dark brown sugar

¾ teaspoon ground cinnamon

Pinch of kosher salt

SIMPLE SYRUP GLAZE

½ cup granulated sugar

FOR SERVING

Roughly chopped pecans

Confectioners' sugar

Michelle Lopez, of desserts and baking blog *Hummingbird High,* baked up this recipe by combining three beloved breakfast treats: babka, morning buns, and cinnamon rolls. It involves yeasted bread, which can be intimidating, but if you remember these three guidelines, you'll be fine. First, do not heat the buttermilk above 110°F. Second, when rolling out the dough, the longer you make your rectangle, the prettier your rolls will be. It doesn't have to be perfect, but try to make twenty inches work. Lastly, it may seem like a lot of sugar syrup, but be patient and keep brushing the buns until they absorb all of the liquid. This little bit of extra effort gives these buns a whole lotta gooey goodness.

Make the dough: In a large bowl, combine the flour, granulated sugar, instant yeast, baking soda, and salt. Set aside.

In the bowl of a stand mixer fitted with the whisk attachment, whisk together the buttermilk, egg, and oil. Add the flour mixture to the bowl and change the whisk attachment to the dough hook. Mix on low speed until the dough is smooth and elastic, about 10 minutes. If the dough is sticky, add flour, 1 tablespoon at a time, until the dough is smooth. If the dough is dry, add more buttermilk, 1 tablespoon at a time.

Transfer the dough to a greased bowl, cover with plastic wrap, and keep in a warm place until the dough has doubled in size, about 1½ hours.

As the dough is rising, prepare the chocolate filling: In the bowl of a food processor, pulse the dark chocolate until it is very finely chopped with some parts almost powdery. Add the butter and pulse until the butter is

continued

evenly distributed. Add the brown sugar, cinnamon, and salt and process until evenly distributed. At this point, you should have a crumbly mixture that resembles clumps of cookie crumbs. Set aside.

Once the dough has doubled in size, transfer it to a lightly floured counter and use a rolling pin to roll it into a rectangle about 12 by 20 inches. Sprinkle the chocolate filling evenly over the surface of the dough, making sure to go right up to the edges of the dough.

Coat a medium cast-iron fry pan with butter. Working widthwise, roll the dough into a log, pinching the edges to seal. Cut the roll into 7 to 9 pieces that are 2 to 2½ inches wide. Place cut-side down in the prepared fry pan in a circle, with one bun in the middle. Cover with plastic wrap and let rise in a warm place until the edges of the rolls are rounded and touching each other, 1 to 1½ hours.

During the second rise, preheat the oven to 350°F.

Bake the buns for 30 to 35 minutes, until the edges of the buns are golden in color. If the tops of the rolls start to brown too quickly, cover with aluminum foil and continue baking until a skewer comes out clean. Let cool on a wire rack until warm.

While the rolls are cooling, make the simple syrup glaze: Combine the sugar and ½ cup water in a petite French oven over high heat. Whisk to dissolve the sugar and bring to a boil. Remove from the heat and use a pastry brush to immediately brush each roll with a generous amount of syrup while the rolls are still warm. It may seem like there is too much syrup for the buns, but just be patient and let the syrup soak in before brushing again. Garnish with pecans and confectioners' sugar and serve warm from the pan.

BUCKWHEAT CREPES WITH EGG, HAM, AND CHEESE

4 large eggs

2 cups whole milk

1½ cups buckwheat flour

½ cup all-purpose flour

¼ cup unsalted butter, melted

2 tablespoons neutral oil

Salt and freshly ground black pepper

FOR SERVING

Grated Gruyère or cheddar cheese

Thinly sliced ham

Fried eggs

Chopped chives (optional)

Sweet crepes filled with berries, sugar, lemon curd, or Nutella get all the glory. How can they not? But savory crepes steal the show when they're made with buckwheat, an earthy flour that imparts a minerally, nutty flavor. Buckwheat's slight bitterness adores the saltiness of ham and cheese, the classic combo from Brittany, where they are known as galettes (not to be confused with the free-form tart on page 185).

The key to making any type of crepe is getting the pan to the right temperature. The sweet spot for this recipe is low to medium-low heat. Just like pancakes, the first one or two crepes are often a bust, so don't despair and just keep cooking.

In a blender, combine the eggs, milk, buckwheat flour, all-purpose flour, melted butter, ½ cup water, and a big pinch of salt and pepper. Blend on high speed until smooth. Let the batter rest in the refrigerator for 30 minutes. Check and add more water if needed so the batter is liquidy like milk rather than thick.

While the batter rests, heat an 11-inch cast-iron crepe pan over low to medium-low heat. Brush the pan with a thin coating of oil. Add ½ cup batter to the center of the pan. Using a crepe tool or by swirling the pan, spread the crepe batter over the entire crepe pan. Cook for 1 to 2 minutes, until the edges of the crepe begin to pull away from the plan, then flip and cook for another minute, until the edges pull away from the sides. Repeat with the remaining batter.

Return a crepe to the warm crepe pan. Add a handful of cheese to the center of the crepe and allow it to melt. Top with a slice of ham, a fried egg, chives, and a pinch of salt and pepper. Fold the edges of the crepe onto the fried egg. Repeat with the remaining crepes and serve immediately.

CINNAMON APPLE PUFFED PANCAKE

FROM TIEGHAN GERARD OF *HALF BAKED HARVEST*

MAKES 4 SERVINGS

PANCAKE

1 firm but crisp apple, such as Honeycrisp or Granny Smith, cut in half, cored, and thinly sliced

6 tablespoons unsalted butter, melted

1 tablespoon brown sugar

4 large eggs

⅔ cup whole milk

⅔ cup all-purpose flour

2 teaspoons vanilla extract

¾ teaspoon ground cinnamon

½ teaspoon salt

CINNAMON MAPLE SYRUP

½ cup maple syrup

2 tablespoons unsalted butter

½ teaspoon ground cinnamon

½ teaspoon vanilla extract

FOR SERVING

Whipped cream (optional)

Tieghan Gerard serves up her tasty blog, *Half Baked Harvest*, from an idyllic Colorado log barn. The self-taught chef learned to cook while preparing meals for her large family. You can taste the love in this recipe, which combines the best fall flavors into one delicious breakfast dish. The result is something between a Dutch baby and apple pie. It is the perfect pancake for a brisk autumn day.

Set an oven rack to the center position and preheat the oven to 425°F.

Make the pancake: Arrange three-quarters of the apple slices in the bottom of a medium cast-iron fry pan and drizzle 4 tablespoons of the butter over the apples. Sprinkle on the brown sugar, place the pan in the oven, and bake for 10 minutes, or until the apples have begun to soften and caramelize.

Meanwhile, in a blender, combine the eggs, milk, flour, vanilla, cinnamon, salt, and the remaining 2 tablespoons melted butter. Blend on high speed for 30 seconds, or until the batter is smooth. Remove the hot fry pan from the oven and pour the batter into the fry pan.

Return the fry pan to the oven and bake for 18 to 20 minutes, until the pancake is puffed and browned on top. Do not open the oven during the first 15 minutes of cooking, or you might deflate the pancake.

While the pancake is baking, make the cinnamon maple syrup: In a petite French oven, combine the maple syrup, butter, and cinnamon and bring to a boil over high heat, whisking until incorporated. Remove from the heat and stir in the vanilla. Set aside, keeping it warm.

Remove the pancake from the oven and top with the remaining apple slices, some whipped cream, and the cinnamon maple syrup. Serve immediately.

SPICY TOFU AND VEGETABLE SCRAMBLE

FROM JEANINE DONOFRIO OF *LOVE & LEMONS*

MAKES 4 TO 6 SERVINGS

I tablespoon olive oil

½ onion, diced

Sea salt

8 ounces cremini mushrooms, thinly sliced

½ red bell pepper, cut into ½-inch pieces

½ green bell pepper, cut into ½-inch pieces

2 cloves garlic, minced

2 chipotle chiles in adobo sauce, chopped

½ teaspoon ground cumin

I pound extra-firm tofu, pressed in paper towels and crumbled

2 green onions, white and light green parts, thinly sliced

I tablespoon fresh lime juice

Freshly ground black pepper

¼ teaspoon ground turmeric (optional, for color)

¾ cup cooked black beans, drained and rinsed

2 cups packed fresh spinach

I cup packed chopped fresh cilantro

FOR SERVING

8 to I0 tortillas, warmed

I avocado, diced, tossed with a squeeze of lime and pinch of sea salt

Your favorite salsa

Helmed by husband-wife-duo Jack Mathews and Jeanine Donofrio, *Love & Lemons* is filled with recipes that are simple, tasty, and healthy. The Chicago-based bloggers make vegetarian dishes dazzle. Case in point, this chipotle, tofu, and vegetable scramble. Filled with lots of hearty vegetables and protein, it is a satisfying breakfast that could easily make a cameo for dinner. The couple adds depth to the scramble with piquant chipotles, aka smoked jalapeños. Look for canned chipotles in the Mexican section of your grocery store—and make sure to serve this scramble with warm tortillas and lots of avocado and salsa.

In a medium cast-iron fry pan, heat the oil over medium heat. Add the onion and a generous pinch of salt and cook, stirring occasionally, until softened, about 3 minutes. Stir in the mushrooms and cook until softened and lightly browned, about 5 more minutes. Stir in the red and green bell peppers and cook for 2 more minutes, or until softened.

Reduce the heat to low and add the garlic, chipotles, and cumin. Stir to incorporate and move to the side of the pan, making room for the tofu. Add the tofu, green onions, lime juice, ½ teaspoon salt, and several grinds of black pepper and stir to combine. If the scramble looks dry, add up to 3 tablespoons water, 1 tablespoon at a time, to moisten.

Cook for 3 more minutes, stirring occasionally, until the mixture is incorporated and the tofu is warm. Stir in the turmeric, black beans, and spinach and cook until the spinach is wilted and the beans are heated through. Remove from the heat and sprinkle with the cilantro. Serve with tortillas, avocado, and salsa.

MIXED-BERRY BAKED OATMEAL

FROM CAMILLE STYLES OF *CAMILLE STYLES*

MAKES 6 TO 8 SERVINGS

2 cups old-fashioned rolled oats

½ cup packed light brown sugar

1 cup chopped walnuts

½ cup unsweetened coconut flakes

1 teaspoon baking powder

1½ teaspoons ground cinnamon

¾ teaspoon salt

2 large eggs

2 cups whole dairy or nondairy milk, such as almond milk

1½ teaspoons vanilla extract

3 tablespoons unsalted butter, melted

2 bananas, sliced

⅔ cup mixed berries such as blueberries, strawberries, and raspberries

FOR SERVING

Crème fraîche or plain Greek yogurt (optional)

Maple syrup

Like the lifestyle blog that shares her name, Camille Styles inspires us with her beautiful, healthy dishes. Her Mixed-Berry Baked Oatmeal is a modern breakfast staple. Made with eggs, milk, and bananas, this version is a cross between bread pudding and banana bread, but since it's made with oats, it is definitely healthier. Packed with nuts and assorted berries, it will give you tons of energy to power through a busy morning.

Styles serves her baked oatmeal topped with crème fraîche or Greek yogurt, adding a drizzle of maple syrup for a hint of sweetness. To make this an easy weekday breakfast, you can assemble the dish the night before, cover with plastic wrap, refrigerate overnight, then pop it in the oven in the morning uncovered.

Preheat the oven to 350°F. Coat an 8 by 12-inch rectangular cast-iron roasting pan with butter or oil.

In a medium bowl, mix together the oats, brown sugar, ¾ cup of the walnuts, ¼ cup of the coconut flakes, the baking powder, cinnamon, and salt. In a separate medium bowl, whisk the eggs, milk, and vanilla. Pour the egg mixture into the dry ingredients, add the melted butter, and stir to combine.

Arrange the sliced bananas in a single even layer over the roasting pan, then sprinkle ⅓ cup of the berries on top. Pour the oat mixture over the bananas and berries, then evenly distribute the remaining ¼ cup walnuts, ¼ cup coconut flakes, and ⅓ cup berries on top of the oats.

Bake for 40 to 45 minutes, or until the top is golden and the oats are set throughout. Serve topped with a dollop of crème fraîche and maple syrup.

KALE SHAKSHUKA WITH GARLIC, FETA, AND LEMON FROM MOLLY YEH OF *MY NAME IS YEH*

2 tablespoons olive oil

6 cloves garlic, minced

1½ teaspoons sweet paprika

1 pound kale, stemmed and coarsely chopped

Kosher salt

½ cup chicken or vegetable stock

4 ounces feta cheese, crumbled

Freshly ground black pepper

Pinch of red pepper flakes

Juice of ½ lemon

6 large eggs

FOR SERVING

Greek yogurt

Za'atar

Chopped fresh flat-leaf parsley

Crusty bread

Shakshuka is a classic recipe that originated in North Africa, but that doesn't mean it can't be tweaked. Instead of using tomatoes, here Molly Yeh, creator of the entertaining blog *My Name is Yeh*, cleverly substitutes kale and lemon to create an earthy and delicious green version. She prefers to serve the dish in individual cocottes, but you could easily swap them for a 12-inch cast-iron fry pan, so that guests eat communally. The perfect pairing is a sizable hunk of crusty bread, for dipping into the runny yolks and sopping up the verdant sauce. Traditionally, shakshuka is eaten for breakfast, but it makes a delightful, and easy, weeknight dinner.

Preheat the oven to 350°F.

In a medium cast-iron cocotte, heat the oil over medium heat. Add the garlic and paprika and cook, stirring, for 30 seconds, then add the kale in two or three batches, allowing it to wilt slightly in between so it can all fit into the pot. Add a good pinch of salt and cook, stirring often, for 7 to 9 minutes, until the kale is softened. Stir in the stock and cook for 5 more minutes, until slightly reduced. Add the cheese, a few turns of black pepper, a pinch of red pepper flakes, and the lemon juice. Taste and adjust the seasoning as desired.

Distribute the kale mixture among 6 mini cocottes and create a well in the center of each. Crack an egg into each well and bake uncovered until the whites are cooked but the yolks are still runny; begin checking for doneness at 12 minutes.

Top each cocotte with a drizzle of yogurt and a sprinkle of za'atar, parsley, salt, and pepper and serve immediately with crusty bread.

GRILLED FRENCH TOAST AND PEACHES WITH WHIPPED CREAM

MAKES 4 TO 6 SERVINGS

2 tablespoons vegetable oil or other neutral oil

4 large eggs

⅓ cup brown sugar

I tablespoon plus I teaspoon vanilla extract

I teaspoon ground cinnamon

1½ cups half-and-half

Pinch of salt

8 (¾-inch-thick) slices challah or brioche bread

2 peaches, cut in half and pitted

I cup heavy cream

2 tablespoons granulated sugar

FOR SERVING

Maple syrup

Cooking French toast on an outdoor grill would leave behind a sticky mess. But in a cast-iron grill pan on the stovetop, you can get maximum caramelization and a hint of smoky flavor—all in the comfort of your indoor kitchen. Brioche or challah are this recipe's best friends—the buttery breads stay crispy on the outside while turning soft and creamy on the inside. Served with grilled peaches and a dollop of whipped cream, this French toast is the ultimate breakfast or brunch treat.

Brush a cast-iron grill pan lightly the with the oil and preheat it over medium-high heat.

In a large, shallow bowl, combine the eggs, brown sugar, 1 tablespoon of the vanilla, the cinnamon, half-and-half, and salt. Whisk well. Working in batches, add 2 or 3 slices of bread to the egg mixture and leave them for a couple minutes to soak up the egg mixture.

Remove the bread slices from the egg mixture, then grill them for about 6 minutes, flipping halfway through, until the egg is set and the toast is golden brown. Remove from the pan and keep warm while you grill the remaining bread.

Wipe the grill pan, add the peaches cut-side down, and grill for 4 to 6 minutes, until they have begun to soften and are slightly charred. Remove the peaches from the pan, thinly slice them, and set aside.

In the bowl of a stand mixer fitted with the whisk attachment, combine the heavy cream, granulated sugar, and the remaining 1 teaspoon vanilla. Whisk on medium high speed until soft peaks form.

Serve the grilled French toast with the peach slices, a dollop of whipped cream, and a drizzle of maple syrup.

SAVORY DUTCH BABY WITH PROSCIUTTO, FONTINA, AND FRIED EGGS

4 large eggs

1 cup whole milk

1 cup all-purpose flour

1 tablespoon chopped fresh chives, plus more for garnish

Pinch of kosher salt and freshly ground black pepper

¼ cup unsalted butter, cut into cubes

½ cup grated Fontina cheese

4 slices prosciutto

3 fried eggs (optional)

Flaky sea salt

A Dutch baby looks like a culinary feat when it emerges fresh from the oven, puffed and golden brown. But the truth is that this tasty popover-meets-pancake couldn't be easier to make. It is a wonderful choice for brunch, as it feeds a crowd all from one pan. Usually Dutch baby recipes skew sweet, but this one leans savory with a mix of herbs, cheese, prosciutto, and, of course, fried eggs.

The batter is best made in a blender for maximum aeration; this gives the pancake that glorious puff. Add the wet ingredients to the blender first; that way the dry ingredients won't clump at the bottom. To make this recipe even easier, you can make the batter the night before and let it hang out in your fridge overnight. It's best to store the batter in the blender, since you'll want to pulse it a few times before cooking your Dutch baby in the morning.

Preheat the oven to 450°F. Slide a medium cast-iron fry pan into the oven to heat while you make the Dutch baby batter.

In a blender, combine the eggs, milk, flour, chives, kosher salt, and pepper. Blend on high speed for about 1 minute, until well combined and frothy.

Using an oven mitt, remove the pan from the oven, add the butter, and let it melt, swirling it to cover the entire pan. Pour the batter into the pan and bake the Dutch baby for 15 to 17 minutes, until puffed and golden brown. Carefully remove the Dutch baby from the oven, sprinkle with the cheese, then return to the oven just until the cheese melts.

Top with the prosciutto and fried eggs. Garnish with chives and a sprinkle of sea salt and serve immediately.

PEANUT BUTTER, CHOCOLATE CHIP, AND COCONUT GRANOLA BARS

MAKES 8 TO 10 BARS

1½ cups raw unsalted almonds

½ cup raw pumpkin seeds

1 cup unsweetened coconut flakes

2½ cups old-fashioned rolled oats

1 cup honey

½ cup creamy unsweetened peanut butter

2 tablespoons coconut oil

1 teaspoon vanilla extract

1 teaspoon almond extract

1 teaspoon kosher salt

½ cup dark chocolate chips

Packed with protein, these wholesome granola bars offer serious snacking power, perfect for a hike, a road trip, or a breakfast that fuels you until dinner. Equally delicious and nutritous, these addictive bars are so simple to make, you might never go back to processed, store-bought ones. The recipe asks for almonds, but you can swap in almost any raw unsalted nuts, such as pecans, cashews, or hazelnuts. If you like your bars thicker and chewier, use a smaller roasting pan. Or, if you prefer them thinner and crispier, opt for a larger one.

Preheat the oven to 350°F.

Lightly oil or butter an 8 by 12-inch rectangular cast-iron roasting pan and line it with parchment paper, leaving a 2-inch overhang on the long sides of the pan.

In a large bowl, combine the almonds, pumpkin seeds, coconut flakes, and oats. Toss well, then spread the mixture over a baking sheet. Toast for 10 to 12 minutes, stirring once or twice, until lightly browned. Let cool slightly, then return to the bowl.

Decrease the oven temperature to 300°F.

In a medium cast-iron fry pan, combine the honey, peanut butter, and oil. Place over medium-low heat and stir until melted and well combined. Let cool slightly, then add the vanilla and almond extracts and salt.

Pour the honey mixture over the oat mixture and stir well to combine. Let cool slightly, then fold in the chocolate chips. Press the mixture into the prepared pan and bake for 20 to 25 minutes, until golden brown. Let cool in the pan completely, then cut into 8 to 10 bars.

ASPARAGUS, CHANTERELLE, AND CHÈVRE FRITTATA WITH CHERVIL

8 large eggs

½ cup half-and-half

1 teaspoon kosher salt

¼ teaspoon freshly ground black pepper, plus more for serving

2 tablespoons olive oil

1 leek, white and light green parts, cut in half and thinly sliced

8 ounces chanterelle mushrooms, sliced if large

1 bunch (about 12 ounces) asparagus, woody ends trimmed and cut into 2-inch pieces

2 cloves garlic, minced

4 ounces chèvre, crumbled

FOR SERVING

Chopped fresh chervil

Flaky sea salt

Frittatas are wonderfully versatile, brilliant for using up leftovers or the season's bounty. This dish takes advantage of the best of spring, with bright asparagus and a garnish of fresh chervil.

Chanterelles are vibrant yellow-orange wild mushrooms with a mild peppery flavor. If you can't find them, oyster mushrooms or even cremini mushrooms are great alternatives. Chervil—which looks a lot like carrot tops—tastes like a blend of parsley and tarragon. It is abundant in the spring, but if you can't find it, opt for parsley instead.

This recipe is a great base on which you can build your own flavor combinations. Consider swapping in any of your favorite ingredients to create your own version. Fast and easy, frittatas are ideal for a weeknight meal. If you manage to have leftovers, they also taste great at room temperature for a portable lunch.

Preheat the oven to 350°F.

In a medium bowl, whisk the eggs, half-and-half, kosher salt, and pepper. Set aside.

Heat the oil in a medium cast-iron fry pan over medium heat. Add leek and cook for about 2 minutes, until softened. Add the mushrooms and cook for 5 minutes, or until softened. Add the asparagus and cook for 3 to 5 minutes, until it turns bright green and begins to soften slightly. Add the garlic and cook for another 30 seconds.

Top the asparagus-mushroom mixture with the egg mixture. Sprinkle with the chèvre and cook the frittata on the stovetop for about 3 minutes, until the sides begin to set. Transfer to the oven and bake for 15 to 20 minutes, until the top is golden brown and the eggs are set. Serve immediately, topped with pepper, chervil, and a sprinkling of flaky sea salt.

VANILLA BEAN OLD-FASHIONED DOUGHNUTS

——— MAKES 8 DOUGHNUTS

BATTER

3 cups all-purpose flour

I teaspoon salt

I tablespoon plus I teaspoon baking powder

¼ teaspoon baking soda

Pinch of freshly grated nutmeg

¾ cup granulated sugar

¼ cup brown sugar

6 tablespoons unsalted butter, at room temperature

2 large eggs

½ cup buttermilk

I tablespoon vanilla bean paste or vanilla extract

Vegetable oil, for frying

GLAZE

I cup powdered sugar

Pinch of salt

½ cup heavy cream, plus more as needed

I tablespoon vanilla bean paste or vanilla extract

If you're looking for a doughnut to dunk in your coffee, this one is for you. Cake doughnuts—unlike their light and airy yeast cousins—are deliciously dense.

Make the batter: In a medium bowl, whisk together the flour, salt, baking powder, baking soda, and nutmeg. Set aside. In the bowl of a stand mixer fitted with a paddle attachment, combine the sugars and butter and mix on medium speed until creamy. Add the eggs one at a time and mix on medium speed until smooth. Add the buttermilk and vanilla bean paste and mix to combine. Slowly add the dry ingredients and mix to combine.

Coat a large bowl with oil, add the batter, cover with plastic wrap, and refrigerate for at least 4 hours, or up to overnight.

Line a baking sheet with parchment paper and set a wire rack into a second baking sheet. Scoop the dough out onto a well-floured surface and roll it out ¾ inch thick. Using a 3½-inch doughnut cutter, cut out doughnut shapes. Place on the prepared baking sheet. Repeat with the remaining dough, rerolling the dough once to get 8 doughnuts. Refrigerate for 30 minutes.

While the dough is chilling, in a medium cast-iron cocotte, add the oil until it comes halfway up the side of the pot. Heat the oil over medium-high heat until it reaches 350°F on a candy thermometer.

Working in batches, add the doughnuts to the oil and fry for 3 to 4 minutes, flipping halfway through, or until the doughnut is golden brown. Let the doughnuts cool on the baking sheet fitted with a rack.

While the doughnuts are cooling, make the glaze: In a medium bowl, combine the powdered sugar, salt, cream, and vanilla bean paste. Stir until smooth, adding more cream if needed. Dunk the doughnuts into the glaze, then set them back on the rack to dry.

SIDES & SALADS

Grilled Romaine with Lemon
and Parmesan 28

Yogurty Beet Salad with Za'atar 31

Thai Flank Steak Salad 32

Freekeh Salad with Caramelized
Onion, Arugula, Dried Cherries,
and Pistachios 34

Creamy Rosemary Polenta 35

Souffléed Stone-Ground Grits
with Aged Cheddar Cheese 36

Mejadra Rice with Lentils, Greek
Yogurt, and Fried Shallots 39

Blistered Padrón Peppers
with Smoked Sea Salt 40

Grilled Carrots
with Bagna Cauda 43

Oven-Roasted Root Vegetables with
Sweet and Sour Mustard Sauce 44

Artichokes à la Barigoule 45

Leek, Parmesan,
and Hazelnut Gratin 46

Whole Roasted Cauliflower
with Herbed Bread Crumbs 49

Kung Pao Cauliflower 50

Roasted Acorn Squash
with Spicy Tahini Yogurt and
Pomegranate Seeds 53

Roasted Brussels Sprouts
with Avocado and Lime 54

Sweet Potatoes Pommes Anna 57

Italian Sausage and Fig Stuffing 58

Pumpkin, Bacon, and Kale Gratin 61

GRILLED ROMAINE WITH LEMON AND PARMESAN

2 heads romaine lettuce, cut in half lengthwise

Olive oil

Salt and freshly ground black pepper

FOR SERVING

½ cup Parmesan cheese, grated

Juice of ½ lemon

2 tablespoons toasted pine nuts

This recipe perfectly illustrates why simple is almost always better. The romaine is lightly grilled to give it a bit of sweetness, then drizzled with lemon juice and topped with Parmesan cheese and toasted pine nuts. It looks fancy, but it's oh-so-easy to make, since tightly packed romaine heads won't fall apart when being flipped. Be sure to grill the romaine just before serving, as it doesn't hold the heat for a long time. This charred romaine can mix up your usual salad routine for family dinner yet is impressive enough to serve to guests. Pair it with Spatchcock Chicken with Fresh Figs and Thyme (page 140).

Generously brush the cut sides of the lettuce with oil and sprinkle with salt and pepper.

Heat a cast-iron grill pan over medium-high heat until just smoking. Grill the lettuce for 5 minutes, flipping halfway through, until the leaves are just barely charred. Top with the cheese, a squeeze of lemon, the pine nuts, and a sprinkle of salt and pepper. Serve immediately.

YOGURTY BEET SALAD WITH ZA'ATAR

FROM NOAH GOLDBERG OF PETER PAN BISTRO

MAKES 6 TO 8 SERVINGS

DRESSING

¼ cup sherry vinegar

¼ cup olive oil

I tablespoon honey

I teaspoon Dijon mustard

Salt and freshly ground
black pepper

SALAD

3½ pounds beets

I cup plain Greek yogurt

2 tablespoons za'atar

I bunch radishes, thinly sliced

I bunch watercress

Salt and freshly ground
black pepper

Known in Toronto for his seasonally driven Canadian cuisine, chef Noah Goldberg brings out the best in beets with this vibrant salad. The beets are roasted for maximum sweetness, then marinated in a sherry-spiked dressing. Combined with creamy yogurt, crunchy radishes, watercress, and za'atar—a Middle Eastern spice blend with dried herbs and sesame seeds—this salad has a ton of texture and flavors that will please even the beet averse. Try to use beets that are roughly the same size to ensure even cooking.

Make the dressing: In a medium bowl, whisk together the vinegar, oil, honey, mustard, and a large pinch each of salt and pepper. Set aside.

Preheat the oven to 350°F.

Make the salad: Scrub the beets under running water and place them in a large cast-iron roasting pan. Add enough water so that the beets are one-third covered with water. Bring the water to a boil over high heat, then remove the pan from the heat, cover with aluminum foil, place in the oven, and roast for about 45 minutes, until a knife inserted into a beet is met without resistance.

Carefully remove the beets from the pan and place them in a bowl. Cover with plastic wrap and let the beets rest for 20 to 30 minutes, until they are cool enough to handle. Remove the skin with a peeler and cut the beets into wedges. Toss the beets in the dressing and allow them to cool, covered, in the refrigerator.

Assemble the salad by placing the marinated beets on a plate, reserving any excess dressing. Dollop the beets with the yogurt, sprinkle with the za'atar, arrange the radishes and watercress around the plate, and finish with a drizzle of the remaining dressing and a sprinkle of salt and pepper. Serve immediately.

THAI FLANK STEAK SALAD

MAKES 4 SERVINGS

I pound flank steak

Salt and freshly ground
black pepper

¼ cup fresh lime juice

3 tablespoons vegetable oil

2 tablespoons fish sauce

2 tablespoons soy sauce

I clove garlic, minced

I Thai bird chile, minced
(optional)

I tablespoon honey

2 heads of Little Gem
or butter lettuce

I cup cherry tomatoes,
cut in half

½ cucumber, thinly sliced

Handful of fresh mint leaves

This salad has all the fresh flavors people love in Thai food—spicy chiles, cooling mint, and pungent fish sauce. When topped with hot-off-the-grill flank steak, the mix of warm and cool ingredients make for a marvelous weeknight meal. If you can't find flank steak, consider swapping in skirt steak and reducing the cooking time to 6 to 8 minutes for medium rare.

Don't worry if you don't have a barbecue. A cast iron grill pan brings the grill indoors; its ridges make grill marks as good as any barbecue can. Enjoy this salad al fresco with a cold Singha, Thailand's popular beer, or a similiarly crisp lager.

Heat a cast-iron grill pan over medium-high heat until just barely smoking. Sprinkle the steak with salt and pepper. Grill the steak for 10 to 12 minutes, flipping halfway through, for medium rare. Remove the steak from the pan to a plate, cover with foil, and let it rest while you assemble the salad dressing.

In a medium bowl, combine the lime juice, oil, fish sauce, soy sauce, garlic, chile, and honey and whisk to dissolve the honey.

Thinly slice the steak against the grain and toss it with half of the salad dressing. Place the steak in a serving bowl and mix with the lettuce, cherry tomatoes, cucumber, mint, and a drizzle of the remaining dressing. Serve warm or at room temperature.

FREEKEH SALAD WITH CARAMELIZED ONION, ARUGULA, DRIED CHERRIES, AND PISTACHIOS

MAKES 4 TO 6 SERVINGS

1½ cups freekeh

½ cup dried sour cherries, roughly chopped

2 tablespoons white wine vinegar

6 tablespoons olive oil, plus more if needed

2 onions, thinly sliced

Salt

2 cups arugula

½ cup roughly chopped fresh basil

½ cup roughly chopped fresh flat-leaf parsley

½ cup roughly chopped fresh mint

½ cup toasted unsalted pistachios, chopped

Freshly ground black pepper

Juice of ½ lemon

This salad was inspired by Yotam Ottolenghi, master of making Middle Eastern grains like freekeh delicious and indulgent. Freekeh, which has a nutty and earthy flavor, can be found in most grocery stores in the grains section, but if you can't find it, replace it with quinoa or wild rice. Ottolenghi's original recipe calls for three types of grains in the salad; here we stick to just one to keep it simple, but we pair it with a riot of flavors from sweet caramelized onion and fresh herbs to spicy arugula and tart dried cherries.

Put the freekeh in a cast-iron petite French oven. Place over low heat and toast for 1 minute. Add 3¼ cups water, increase the heat to high, and bring to a boil. Reduce the heat to low, cover, and cook until the water is absorbed, about 20 minutes. Remove from the heat and let sit for 20 minutes at room temperature. Using a fork, carefully fluff the freekeh and let cool until warm.

Meanwhile, in a small bowl, combine the sour cherries and vinegar. Set aside while you cook the onion.

In a 4-quart cast-iron cocotte, combine 2 tablespoons of the olive oil, the onions, and a pinch of salt. Cook over low heat for 30 minutes, stirring occasionally, until the onions are caramelized.

Assemble the salad by placing the freekeh in a large bowl. Fold in the cherries and their soaking liquid, the arugula, basil, parsley, mint, and pistachios. Add a big pinch of salt and pepper, the lemon juice, and the remaining 4 tablespoons of olive oil. Taste and add more salt and pepper, if needed, and add more oil if the freekeh is dry. Serve at room temperature.

CREAMY ROSEMARY POLENTA

2 cups whole milk

I teaspoon kosher salt

¾ cup polenta

¼ cup unsalted butter, cut into cubes

½ cup grated Parmesan cheese

I teaspoon chopped fresh rosemary

Flaky sea salt

Polenta has the same reputation as risotto: in order to get a creamy texture, you must constantly stir it. But that doesn't have to be the case. You can cook polenta slowly on the stovetop *without* stirring. The result is a creamy and smooth polenta without all the work. Cast iron is key in this no-stir method, since it evenly retains the low heat to ensure perfectly cooked polenta. Consider topping your polenta with wilted greens and a poached egg, or serve it with Beef Bourguignon (page 125) or Spatchcock Chicken with Fresh Figs and Thyme (page 140).

In a cast-iron petite French oven, combine the milk, 1 cup water, and kosher salt and bring to a simmer over medium heat. Add the polenta to the liquid, stirring constantly. Continue stirring until the polenta has absorbed the liquid and has thickened, 2 to 3 minutes.

Reduce the heat to very low and top the polenta with the butter. Cook without stirring for 1 hour, or until the polenta is creamy. Fold in the cheese and rosemary and serve topped with a sprinkle of flaky sea salt.

SOUFFLÉED STONE-GROUND GRITS WITH AGED CHEDDAR CHEESE FROM JUSTIN DEVILLIER OF LA PETITE GROCERY

MAKES 6 TO 8 SERVINGS

1 cup whole milk

¼ cup unsalted butter

1 teaspoon plus a pinch of salt

Pinch of freshly ground black pepper

1 cup stone-ground grits

2 cups grated aged white cheddar cheese

4 large eggs, separated

Grits can be prepared simply—just ground corn, salt, and butter—but they become transcendent when given an elevated treatment. In this recipe, Justin Devillier, the chef/owner of La Petite Grocery in New Orleans, puts a French spin on the Southern classic. He uses the traditional French technique of incorporating whipped egg whites to add volume—this same method is used to puff up soufflés. Devillier then folds in aged cheddar to spread extra flavor evenly throughout the grits.

Preheat the oven to 350°F.

Combine 2 cups water, the milk, butter, 1 teaspoon salt, and the pepper in a 4-quart cast-iron cocotte. Place over medium-high heat and heat until it is steaming but not quite boiling. Add the grits in a slow, steady stream while whisking to prevent lumps from forming. Once all of the grits are in, bring to a boil, then immediately reduce the heat to low. Cook, stirring occasionally, for about 20 minutes, until the grits are thickened enough to stick to the spoon but not the bottom of the pot. Add the cheese and fold it in to incorporate. Remove from the the heat.

Place the egg whites into the bowl of a stand mixer fitted with the whisk attachment. Add a pinch of salt and whisk on high speed until stiff peaks form. Fold the egg yolks into the warm grits. Add one-quarter of the egg whites and use a spatula to very gently fold them into the grits. Add the remaining whites and fold to combine. If you are using mini cocottes, pour the mixture into the 6 to 8 cocottes, leaving an inch at the top for the soufflé to rise. Bake for 45 minutes for the large cocotte and 30 minutes for the minis, or until puffed up, golden brown on top, and the aroma of toasted cheddar fills the kitchen.

Serve warm.

MEJADRA RICE WITH LENTILS, GREEK YOGURT, AND FRIED SHALLOTS FROM STUART CAMERON OF BYBLOS AND PATRIA

MAKES 4 SERVINGS

½ cup green lentils

2 bay leaves

1 teaspoon salt

2 tablespoons olive oil

½ onion, thinly sliced

¼ teaspoon ground turmeric

½ teaspoon ground allspice

½ teaspoon ground cinnamon

½ teaspoon sugar

⅔ cup basmati rice

FOR SERVING

Plain Greek yogurt

Crispy shallots

Ground cayenne

Chervil leaves

Pivotal in starting the "Middleterranean" cuisine movement in Toronto, chef Stuart Cameron magically marries foreign flavors at his restaurants, Byblos and Patria. Here, he shares his mouthwatering *mejadra* recipe, lentils and rice cooked with warming spices and topped with yogurt and crispy shallots. This ultimate bowl of healthy comfort food is adored across the Arab world. You can find crispy shallots at most Asian grocery stores, or stock up on the packaged fried onions sold at regular grocery stores around the holidays. Make sure to save some of the flavorful broth from the lentils to cook the rice.

Put the lentils in a cast-iron petite French oven, add water to cover, then add the bay leaves and salt. Place over medium heat, bring to a low boil, and boil for 12 to 15 minutes, until the lentils have softened but still have a little bite. Drain, reserving ¾ cup of the cooking water.

Heat the oil in a 4-quart cast-iron cocotte and add the onion. Cook over medium heat, stirring occasionally, until the onion takes on a golden brown color. Add the turmeric, allspice, cinnamon, and sugar and cook for 30 seconds. Add the rice and stir to coat. Add the cooked lentils and reserved lentil stock and bring to a boil. Reduce the heat to very low, cover, and simmer for 11 minutes. Remove from the heat and cover the pot with a clean, dry tea towel. Seal tightly with the lid and set aside for 10 minutes to let the rice rest and absorb all the flavors.

Serve the rice topped with yogurt, crispy shallots, a sprinkle of cayenne, and chervil.

BLISTERED PADRÓN PEPPERS WITH SMOKED SEA SALT

2 tablespoons olive oil

12 ounces Padrón peppers

Smoked flaky sea salt

At the end of summer, peppers pop up in farmers' markets across the country. One to look out for is the Padrón, a small, dark green pepper that rates low on the spice spectrum. These peppers benefit from a bit of blistering heat, lending them a smokiness to complement their soft spice. Serve them as an appetizer at your next barbecue. Caution: they can be addictive, so be sure to make enough. Smoked sea salt can be bought at some grocery stores and specialty markets. If you can't find Padrón peppers, you can substitute shishito peppers.

In a large cast-iron fry pan, heat the oil over medium-high heat until very hot but not smoking. Add the peppers in a single layer and allow them to blister for 3 to 5 minutes, tossing occasionally until slightly charred and tender. Remove the peppers from the pan, place in a bowl, and sprinkle with salt. Serve immediately.

GRILLED CARROTS WITH BAGNA CAUDA

BAGNA CAUDA

6 cloves garlic, minced

½ cup olive oil

8 anchovy fillets, minced

I teaspoon capers, minced

2 tablespoons unsalted butter

2 teaspoons lemon zest

CARROTS

8 ounces small carrots, cut in half if thick

2 tablespoons olive oil

Salt and freshly ground black pepper

Chopped fresh flat-leaf parsley, for garnish

Bagna cauda may sound fancy, but this pungent and flavor-packed Italian sauce is easy to make with just a few ingredients. Traditional bagna cauda, "hot bath" in Italian, is made with garlic, olive oil, anchovies, and butter heated up for a pungent dipping sauce. We add capers and lemon zest to ours for added brightness and balance. Even if you don't like anchovies, you should try them in this recipe, as they give it a satisfying umami punch rather than a fishy flavor. The extra step of blanching the carrots before grilling enables them to cook more evenly for perfect texture and snap. Consider using this bagna cauda as a drizzle on any grilled vegetables. These carrots would be a nice complement to an Italian meal. Or why not try them alongside Grilled Bone-In Rib Eye Topped with Shallot Compote and Watercress (page 171).

Make the bagna cauda: In a petite French oven, combine the garlic, oil, anchovies, capers, and butter and cook over low heat for 15 minutes, or until the garlic is softened. Remove from the heat and fold in the lemon zest.

Prepare the carrots: Bring a large cast-iron cocotte of water to a boil and fill a bowl with ice and water to make an ice-water bath. Add the carrots to the boiling water and blanch for 5 to 8 minutes, until crisp-tender. Drain and place the carrots in the ice-water bath, then drain again and dry them really well.

Heat a cast-iron grill pan over medium-high heat until barely smoking. Toss the carrots with the oil, season with salt and pepper, and grill for 8 to 12 minutes, until lightly charred and fork-tender. Serve warm with a drizzle of the bagna cauda and a garnish of parsley.

OVEN-ROASTED ROOT VEGETABLES WITH SWEET AND SOUR MUSTARD SAUCE FROM NIK SHARMA OF A BROWN TABLE

MAKES 6 SERVINGS

ROASTED VEGETABLES

I pound carrots, cut into 2-inch pieces

I pound parsnips, cut into 2-inch pieces

I pound new potatoes, cut in half

I pound baby beets, peeled and quartered

I onion, thinly sliced

6 cloves garlic, minced

Kosher salt

Freshly ground black pepper

¼ cup olive oil

2 tablespoons chopped fresh flat-leaf parsley, for garnish

SWEET AND SOUR MUSTARD SAUCE

I cup Dijon mustard

¼ cup maple syrup

2 tablespoons mirin

½ teaspoon kosher salt

½ teaspoon freshly ground black pepper

Nik Sharma from the blog *A Brown Table* is known for taking traditional recipes from North India and Goa and adding his unique, personal spin. In this recipe, he roasts root vegetables for caramelized, concentrated flavor. He tosses them with a delicious mustard sauce that is pepped up by mirin (Japanese rice wine) and maple syrup for a salty, sweet, and sour drizzle that hits every note. Consider roasting your beets in a separate pan, as they have the tendency to turn the other vegetables red.

Preheat the oven to 400°F.

Make the roasted vegetables: Place the carrots, parsnips, potatoes, beets, onion, and garlic in a large bowl. Season with salt and pepper and add the oil. Toss to evenly coat and transfer the vegetables to an 8 by 12-inch cast-iron roasting pan. Roast, stirring occasionally, for about 45 minutes, until the vegetables are tender and slightly caramelized.

While the vegetables are roasting, make the sauce: In a small bowl, whisk together the mustard, maple syrup, mirin, kosher salt, and pepper. Set aside.

Place the roasted vegetables in a serving bowl. Garnish with the parsley, drizzle with as much of the mustard sauce as you like, and serve. Extra mustard sauce will keep covered in the refrigerator for up to 1 month.

ARTICHOKES À LA BARIGOULE

FROM JOSEPH KELLER OF THE COMPANY OF THE CAULDRON

MAKES 6 SERVINGS

TOMATO COULIS

1 tablespoon olive oil

½ onion, thinly sliced

1½ pounds tomatoes, seeded

1 tablespoon sugar

Salt and freshly ground black pepper

ARTICHOKES

4 cloves garlic

1 sprig basil, plus chopped basil for garnish

1 sprig flat-leaf parsley, plus chopped parsley for garnish

1 lemon, cut in half

6 artichokes

3 tablespoons olive oil

1 onion, thinly sliced

2 carrots, thinly sliced

½ bay leaf

1 sprig thyme

1 bulb fennel, cored and thinly sliced

Salt and freshly ground black pepper

⅓ cup dry white wine

About 1 cup chicken stock

Chopped fresh cilantro, for garnish

À la barigoule is a Provençal preparation in which the artichokes are braised in white wine and chicken stock. Topped with a delicate tomato coulis, this dish is a fresh and healthy take on comfort food.

Make the tomato coulis: Heat the oil in a large cast-iron fry pan over medium-high heat. Add the onion and cook for 3 to 4 minutes, until softened. Reserve 4 tomato quarters for garnish. Stir the remaining tomatoes and the sugar into the onion. Season with salt and pepper, bring to a simmer, then reduce the heat to medium-low and simmer 15 to 20 minutes. Tranfer to a blender and blend until smooth, then drain the tomato mixture. Taste and add more salt and pepper if needed.

Prepare the artichokes: Chop 2 of the garlic cloves. Place them in a small bowl, add the basil and parsley sprigs, and set aside.

Fill a large bowl with cold water and squeeze 1 lemon half into the water. Trim the leaves at the base of the artichokes and trim the end of the stalks, leaving about 1 inch of the stalk. Rub each artichoke with the second lemon half and plunge the artichokes into the cold water. Take the artichokes out of the water and remove the outer leaves. Scoop out the choke with a teaspoon. Return the artichokes to the water.

Heat the oil in a large rectangular cast-iron roasting pan over medium-high heat. Add the onion and carrots and cook 2 to 3 minutes. Arrange the artichokes in the pan, add the remaining 2 garlic cloves, the bay leaf, thyme, and fennel. Season with salt and pepper. Pour in the wine and bring to a boil for 15 seconds. Add enough stock to barely cover the artichokes. Cover the pan, reduce the heat to medium, and cook for 15 minutes, or until the stalks are fork-tender. Add the chopped garlic, basil, and parsley mixture to the artichokes and mix well. Transfer to a serving bowl and top with the braising sauce and the tomato coulis. Garnish with the reserved tomato quarters and the chopped parsley, cilantro, and basil.

LEEK, PARMESAN, AND HAZELNUT GRATIN

FROM ERIK ANDERSON OF COI

12 leeks, cleaned and trimmed to about 6 inches

2¼ cups heavy cream

½ cup unsalted butter

3 cloves garlic, peeled

6 sprigs thyme

¾ cup plus 2 tablespoons whole toasted and peeled hazelnuts

2 cups grated Parmesan cheese

Salt and freshly ground black pepper

Fresh lemon juice, if needed

2 tablespoons panko bread crumbs

1 teaspoon chopped fresh chives

Chef Erik Anderson, of Coi in San Francisco, takes the humble leek and elevates it in this decadent gratin. He adds crunch with panko bread crumbs, texture with hazelnuts, and flavor with garlic and thyme. Creamy and crunchy with a gorgeous golden-brown crust, it's brilliant in its simplicity. Pair with Black Pepper and Porcini–Crusted Filet with Herbed Butter (page 168) or Braised Chicken Thighs with Mushrooms and Madeira (page 142) for a mouthwatering meal.

Preheat the oven to 375°F.

Bring a large cast-iron cocotte of water to a boil and fill a bowl with ice and water to make an ice-water bath. Add the leeks to the boiling water and cook until bright green and slightly softened, 2 to 3 minutes. Shock the leeks in the ice-water bath to prevent further cooking. Drain and set aside.

In a medium cast-iron cocotte, combine the cream, butter, garlic, thyme, and ¾ cup whole hazelnuts. Bring to a boil, then reduce the heat to low and simmer for 30 minutes for the flavors to combine. Remove thyme sprigs, then transfer to a blender and blend until smooth. Fold in the cheese. Season with salt and pepper and add a little lemon juice, if needed.

Place the leeks in a large oval cast-iron roasting or fry pan and cover with the cream mixture. Sprinkle the panko over the top and bake for 30 to 40 minutes, until golden brown and bubbly. Chop the remaining hazelnuts then sprinkle over gratin along with chives and serve.

WHOLE ROASTED CAULIFLOWER
WITH HERBED BREAD CRUMBS

1 head cauliflower (2 to 2½ pounds), stem removed but florets kept intact

5 tablespoons olive oil

Salt and freshly ground black pepper

¾ cup panko bread crumbs

1 tablespoon chopped fresh thyme

½ lemon

When you roast cauliflower whole, it deepens in flavor and becomes crispy and tender at the same time. Whole roasting elevates the brassica to main-course status—you won't miss the meat in this hearty preparation. Herbed bread crumbs give the cauliflower a crunchy texture boost. Take care when you add the bread crumbs to the cauliflower, as both the pan and the cauliflower will be very hot. It's fine if some of the bread-crumb mixture falls to the bottom of the pan; simply spoon it on top of the cauliflower as you serve it.

Preheat the oven to 425°F.

Drizzle the whole cauliflower with 2 tablespoons of the oil and a sprinkle of salt and pepper. Place the cauliflower in a cast-iron fry pan, cover with aluminum foil, and bake for 30 minutes. Remove the foil and bake for another 50 minutes, or until cauliflower is fork-tender.

While the cauliflower is roasting, in a medium bowl, mix together the remaining 3 tablespoons oil, the panko, and thyme and season with salt and pepper.

Carefully remove the cauliflower from the oven and sprinkle with the bread-crumb mixture. Using a spatula, gently press the bread crumbs into the cauliflower. Return to the oven and roast for another 10 minutes, or until the bread crumbs are golden. Remove from the oven and let cool slightly. Squeeze the lemon over the cauliflower and carefully remove it from the pan, scooping up extra bread crumbs from the bottom. Taste and add more salt and pepper if needed. Slice and serve.

KUNG PAO CAULIFLOWER

MAKES 6 TO 8 SERVINGS

5 tablespoons soy sauce

3 tablespoons rice wine

I tablespoon cornstarch

I tablespoon hoisin sauce

I tablespoon toasted
sesame oil

2 teaspoons sugar

4 tablespoons vegetable oil

I head cauliflower, stem
removed and cut into
small florets

2 dried red chiles,
or more to taste

2 cloves garlic, minced

½ cup finely chopped
green onions

I tablespoon grated
peeled fresh ginger

¼ cup roasted
unsalted peanuts

Fresh cilantro,
for garnish

Kung pao chicken is a beloved Chinese takeout classic, but it can
be cloying and heavy. This version reduces the sugar and ups the
powerful aromatics, like ginger, garlic, and chile, for a vibrant sauce
that will make your mouth sing. The chicken is swapped for hearty but
lighter cauliflower. Most of the ingredients for this dish can be found
in a grocery store, but make sure you use rice wine, not rice wine
vinegar. Be careful not to overcook the cauliflower and do try to serve
this dish right away, as the moisture in the cauliflower can cause the
sauce to become too liquidy.

In a medium bowl, combine 3 tablespoons of the soy sauce with
2 tablespoons of the rice wine. Whisk in the cornstarch to dissolve and
set aside.

In a small bowl, whisk together the remaining 2 tablespoons soy sauce,
the remaining 1 tablespoon rice wine, the hoisin sauce, sesame oil, and
sugar. Set aside.

In a large cast-iron fry pan or wok, heat 2 tablespoons of the vegetable oil
over medium-high heat. Add the cauliflower to the wok and cook until
it begins to soften and brown, 5 to 7 minutes. Remove the cauliflower to
the bowl with the corn starch mixture. Stir well to coat the cauliflower.

Add the remaining 2 tablespoons vegetable oil to the pan, add the chiles,
and fry until fragrant, about 1 minute. Remove the chiles from the pan to
a small bowl and set aside. Return the cauliflower to the pan, draining any
excess marinade. Cook the cauliflower until it is browned and fork-tender,
5 to 7 minutes. Add the garlic, green onions, ginger, and peanuts and cook
for 1 minute. Remove the pan from the heat, drizzle in the remaining soy
sauce mixture, and toss well. Serve immediately, garnished with cilantro.

ROASTED ACORN SQUASH WITH SPICY TAHINI YOGURT AND POMEGRANATE SEEDS

½ teaspoon ground cinnamon

¼ teaspoon chili powder

Pinch of ground allspice

1 teaspoon plus a pinch of kosher salt

Freshly ground black pepper

6 tablespoons olive oil

1 acorn squash (1½ to 2 pounds), cut into wedges, seeds removed but skin left on

¾ cup plain Greek yogurt

1 teaspoon Aleppo pepper, plus more for finishing

1 teaspoon honey

1 teaspoon fresh lemon juice

1 tablespoon tahini

½ cup roughly chopped fresh mint

½ cup pomegranate seeds

Chopped roasted almonds, for garnish

Flaky sea salt

Spice up your usual squash repetoire with this Middle Eastern–inspired dish brimming with fresh mint, spicy yogurt, and tangy pomegranate seeds. Acorn squash, the squat, dark green-skinned squash that is named for its acorn shape, is in the same family as butternut squash but is a little easier to handle since you don't need to peel it before cooking. Roasting it with the skin on not only saves prep time but also keeps the squash tender and moist. Aleppo pepper is a Middle Eastern spice that is both bright and earthy; if it's unavailable, you can substitute more chili powder or red pepper flakes. This colorful dish is great as a vegetarian main or a hearty side to brighten up a wintry, gray day.

Preheat the oven to 425°F.

In a small bowl, combine the cinnamon, chili powder, allspice, 1 teaspoon kosher salt, and black pepper to taste. Add the squash to a large bowl and toss well with the olive oil. Sprinkle in the spice mixture and stir to ensure that each wedge is covered in spices.

Arrange the squash on a large rectangular cast-iron roasting pan in a single layer. Roast for 35 to 40 minutes, until fork-tender.

While squash is roasting, in a medium bowl, whisk the yogurt with the Aleppo pepper, honey, lemon juice, tahini, a pinch of kosher salt, and black pepper to taste.

Transfer the squash to a platter and drizzle the yogurt mixture over the squash. Top with the mint, pomegranate seeds, almonds, black pepper, and a sprinkle of sea salt. Serve warm.

ROASTED BRUSSELS SPROUTS WITH AVOCADO AND LIME FROM DAN KLUGER OF LORING PLACE

MAKES 4 TO 6 SERVINGS

BRUSSELS SPROUTS

Kosher salt

2 pounds medium brussels sprouts, cut in half through the root end

¼ cup olive oil

Pinch of freshly ground black pepper

DRESSING

¼ cup fresh lime juice

¼ cup olive oil

1 tablespoon Dijon mustard

1 teaspoon whole-grain mustard

2 teaspoons honey

1½ teaspoons Tabasco sauce

A large pinch of kosher salt

1 tablespoon olive oil

½ cup roughly chopped fresh basil

¼ cup roughly chopped fresh mint

2 tablespoons toasted sunflower seeds

½ red finger chile, thinly sliced

½ large avocado, sliced

Zest of 1 lime

Flaky sea salt and freshly ground black pepper

Dan Kluger, chef and owner of the New York City restaurant Loring Place, focuses on channeling seasonal flavors in unexpected yet delightful ways. This recipe is a prime example—the textures of the brussels sprouts and avocado work amazingly well, and a pop of lime, chile, and fresh herbs brings the flavors together in this vibrant and earthy side dish. Gorgeously green, this inventive salad will liven up your dinner table.

Prepare the brussels sprouts: Fill a bowl with ice and water to create an ice-water bath. Bring a large cast-iron cocotte of water to a boil and salt it. Add the brussels sprouts and cook for about 2 minutes, until tender but not fully cooked. Drain, then shock them in the ice water. Drain again and dry on paper towels.

Preheat the oven to 400°F.

Heat the oil in a large cast-iron fry pan over medium-high heat. Add brussels sprouts and 1 tablespoon salt and stir to coat the brussels sprouts in the oil. Place in the oven and roast for 5 to 8 minutes, stirring occasionally, until browned and evenly roasted. Remove from the oven and transfer the brussels sprouts to a paper towel–lined plate.

Make the dressing: In a medium bowl, whisk the lime juice, oil, mustards, honey, Tabasco sauce, and salt. Set aside.

Add the oil to the pan that the brussels sprouts were roasted in and heat over medium-high heat. Add the basil, mint, sunflower seeds, and chile and quickly fry for about 30 seconds.

Place the brussels sprouts on a serving platter and top with the avocado. Drizzle about 3 tablespoons of the dressing over the top, garnish with the herb and seed mixture, and finish with the lime zest and a pinch of flaky sea salt and black pepper.

SWEET POTATOES POMMES ANNA

2 pounds sweet potatoes, peeled

½ cup unsalted butter

2 tablespoons brown sugar

½ teaspoon five-spice powder

I teaspoon salt, plus more for sprinkling

Pinch of freshly ground black pepper

The iconic sweet potato casserole is elevated by a nineteenth century French recipe. Marshmallows are replaced by a bit of brown sugar, and the warming notes of five-spice powder complement the sugariness of the sweet potatoes. It is perfect for a Sunday supper, or layering the sweet potatoes in a circular flower shape makes a pretty presentation for your holiday table. When sliced, each potato slice is addictively crunchy on top and tender in the middle. If you don't have five-spice powder, feel free to substitute cinnamon. These pommes Anna go well with roast turkey or ham or Cider-Brined Pork Chops with Apples and Balsamic Vinegar (page 161).

Preheat the oven 425°F.

Using a knife or mandoline, thinly slice the sweet potatoes ⅛ inch thick. Place the slices in a large bowl.

In a small cast-iron fry pan, combine the butter, brown sugar, five-spice powder, salt, and pepper. Place over medium heat and stir until the butter is completely melted.

Toss the butter mixture with the sweet potatoes, making sure the sweet potatoes are evenly coated. Arrange the sweet potatoes in a single layer in a medium oval cast-iron roasting pan or fry pan, overlapping the slices slightly. Sprinkle with salt. Bake for 40 to 45 minutes, until the potatoes are fork-tender and the edges are golden brown. Serve warm.

ITALIAN SAUSAGE AND FIG STUFFING

MAKES 6 TO 8 SERVINGS

2 tablespoons olive oil

8 ounces Italian sausage, casings removed

1 onion, diced

3 celery stalks, diced

Salt and freshly ground black pepper

¼ cup brandy

6 ounces dried figs, cut in half

2 cups chicken stock

1 teaspoon fresh thyme leaves, chopped, plus more for garnish

1 pound crusty bread, such as ciabatta or French bread, crusts removed and cut into 1-inch cubes

¼ cup heavy cream

Italian cuisine is centered around using a few high-quality ingredients really, really well. That is the inspiration behind this stuffing, in which Italian sausage and dried figs play off each other in salty-sweet harmony. Serve with Turkey Roulade with Sage and Orange (page 147) for a festive holiday menu that goes beyond the usual suspects. Or why not make this as a weeknight side when you want to use up leftover bread?

Preheat oven to 375°F.

In a medium cast-iron roasting pan or braiser, heat the oil over medium heat. Add the sausage and cook, stirring to break it apart, for 5 to 7 minutes, until cooked through. Place the sausage in a large bowl. Add the onion, celery, and a large pinch of salt and pepper to the roasting pan and cook for 5 to 7 minutes, until the onion is translucent and the celery is softened. Deglaze the pan with the brandy and add the figs and stock. Reduce the heat to low and cook for 2 to 3 minutes, until the figs are rehydrated. Stir in the thyme.

Add the bread to the bowl with the sausage, then carefully fold in the fig and vegetable mixture using a large spoon or spatula. Return the bread and sausage mixture to the roasting pan, drizzle with the cream, and top with a sprinkle of salt and pepper.

Cover the roasting pan with aluminum foil and bake for 30 minutes. Remove the foil and bake for another 10 minutes, or until the stuffing is browned on top. Remove from the oven and serve.

PUMPKIN, BACON, AND KALE GRATIN

FROM PAUL VIRANT OF VIE AND VISTRO

¼ cup diced bacon

2 cloves garlic, minced

I shallot, minced

2 teaspoons chopped fresh thyme

I pound pumpkin, peeled, seeded, and sliced ¼ inch thick

I bunch Tuscan kale, stems removed, roughly chopped, and blanched

2 cups heavy cream

½ cup grated Parmesan cheese

½ cup shredded Gruyère cheese

Salt and freshly ground black pepper

Paul Virant has two restaurants in the Chicago area, where he makes stellar food with a local, seasonal focus. Named after the French verb *gratiner*, which means "to broil," a gratin is essentially any vegetable baked in a shallow dish that develops a crispy crust thanks to its cheese or bread topping. Paul's simple vegetable gratin is easy to assemble and wonderfully indulgent, thanks to bacon, cream, and two kinds of cheeses. Cast-iron allows you to prep and bake the ingredients in the same pan, so you don't lose any delicious bits by moving them between pans. Best enjoyed when the temperature drops, this hearty gratin can be served as a main course with a simple green salad or as a side dish for Roast Chicken with Fingerling Potatoes, Herbs, and Lemon (page 144).

Preheat the oven to 375°F.

Bring a large cast-iron cocotte of salted water to boil. Add the kale and blanch for 2 to 3 minutes or until kale is bright green. Remove and place in an ice bath to stop the cooking. Remove kale from ice bath, then squeeze to remove any excess liquid.

In a medium cast-iron roasting or fry pan, cook the bacon over medium heat until crisp, 3 to 5 minutes. Add the garlic, shallot, and thyme and cook for another 30 seconds. Add the pumpkin and kale and mix well.

In a petite French oven, bring the cream to a boil over medium-high heat. Immediately remove the cream from the heat and pour it over the vegetable mixture. Top with the cheeses. Bake until the pumpkin is tender and the cheese is browned, 30 to 40 minutes. Remove from the oven and serve.

BREADS, STARTERS & PASTAS

Baked Ricotta with Chives 67

Grilled Halloumi with
Baba Ghanoush and Dukkah 68

Gruyère Cheese Fondue 71

Toasty Honey Corn Loaf 72

Grilled Flatbread 74

Garlic and Herb Parker House
Rolls 77

No-Knead Cast-Iron Bread 78

Broccoli Rabe Pizza with Caramelized
Onions and Burrata 81

Grilled Cheese with Fig Preserves,
Sage, Prosciutto, and Brie 85

Brown Rice Bowl with Arugula
Pesto, Preserved Lemon, and
Roasted Beets 86

Summertime Pasta with Tomatoes
and Charred Corn 88

Oven-Baked Risotto with Lemon,
Asparagus, and Egg Yolk 91

Triple Crème Mac and Cheese 92

One-Pan Wild Mushroom Lasagna 94

Three Cheese and Spinach
Stuffed Shells 95

Gingery Vietnamese Chicken with
Noodles 96

One-Pot Orecchiette with Swiss
Chard, Sausage, and Lemon 99

Pork Ragù with Pappardelle 100

BAKED RICOTTA WITH CHIVES

FROM JULIA SULLIVAN OF HENRIETTA RED

1 quart whole milk ricotta

4 large eggs, lightly beaten

1 cup grated Parmesan cheese

2 tablespoons chopped fresh chives

Pinch of kosher salt and freshly ground black pepper

2 tablespoons olive oil

½ cup chopped fresh flat-leaf parsley (optional)

2 teaspoons flaky sea salt

FOR SERVING

Toasted crusty sourdough bread

Radishes

At Julia Sullivan's Nashville restaurant, Henrietta Red, the hometown chef focuses on fresh, simple ingredients. In this recipe, ricotta, eggs, and Parmesan are blended and baked together for a gooey, yet gourmet, cheese dip. Inspired by the low-country hospitality that welomes each customer, this recipe works equally well as an appetizer at a cocktail party or as a side dish with dinner.

Preheat the oven to 425°F.

In a medium bowl, fold together the ricotta, eggs, Parmesan cheese, chives, kosher salt, and pepper.

Pour the ricotta mixture into a petite French oven and bake for 55 to 60 minutes, until the top is golden brown and the edges are bubbling. Let rest for 5 minutes, then drizzle with the oil and sprinkle with the parsley and flaky sea salt. Serve immediately with bread and radishes.

GRILLED HALLOUMI WITH BABA GHANOUSH AND DUKKAH FROM THEA BAUMANN, CO-AUTHOR OF *IT'S ALL EASY*

MAKES 4 TO 6 SERVINGS

BABA GHANOUSH

1 medium eggplant

Zest and juice of 1 lemon

1 medium clove garlic, grated

1 tablespoon tahini

3 tablespoons olive oil, plus more for drizzling

Salt

DUKKAH

½ cup peeled hazelnuts, finely chopped

2 tablespoons sesame seeds

¼ teaspoon ground cumin

¼ teaspoon ground coriander

Salt

1 (8.8-ounce) package halloumi cheese, cut into ½-inch slices

Olive oil

Torn fresh mint leaves

If you haven't tried halloumi, you should give this recipe a test drive. Halloumi is a semi hard, brined Greek cheese made from a mixture of goat's milk and sheep's milk. It has a high melting point, which allows it to stand up to grilling, leaving it crisp outside and gooey inside. For this recipe, chef Thea Baumann, contributor to the hub of healthy wellness, *Goop*, tops her halloumi with homemade baba ghanoush and dukkah, a fragrant, nutty Egyptian spice mixture. Serve as a savory appetizer or as a light lunch paired with a green salad.

Make the baba ghanoush: Place the eggplant directly over a gas flame on the stovetop and roast for 15 to 20 minutes, turning with tongs to get an even char. Remove the eggplant to a bowl and cover with plastic wrap.

When the eggplant is cool enough to handle, cut it in half and scoop the flesh into a bowl. Add the lemon zest and juice, garlic, tahini, and oil. Season with salt and stir to combine.

Make the dukkah: Toast the hazelnuts in a medium cast-iron fry pan over medium heat until just beginning to brown, about 3 minutes. Add the sesame seeds and toast for 1 minute more. Add the ground spices and a large pinch of salt and toast for another 30 seconds. Remove to a bowl to cool.

When it is time to serve, heat a cast-iron grill pan over medium-high heat.

Brush the halloumi slices with oil and grill for about 2 minutes per side, or until golden brown and grill marks show. Place on a serving platter. Serve with a large spoonful of the baba ghanoush and sprinkle the dukkah on top. Lightly drizzle oil over the entire dish and garnish with torn mint leaves. Serve immediately.

GRUYÈRE CHEESE FONDUE

MAKES 4 TO 6 SERVINGS

I pound Gruyère cheese, grated

2 tablespoons cornstarch

I tablespoon unsalted butter

2 shallots, finely minced

1¼ cups white wine

I teaspoon Dijon mustard

I tablespoon fresh lemon juice

Pinch of freshly grated nutmeg

Salt and freshly ground black pepper

FOR SERVING

Cubed or grilled bread (optional)

Apple slices (optional)

Blanched or raw vegetables (optional)

Fondue is the traditional après-ski dish in the Alps, devoured after a day in the snow to warm the body from within. It is one of simplest but most satisfying dishes out there. What's not to love about a communal meal among friends dipping bread into warm, gooey cheese? Adding apples and blanched vegetables helps round out the flavors of this rich, indulgent dish. Don't skimp on the cheese—it is important to use the high-quality stuff here. And opt for a chewy, firm bread, like a good baguette or sourdough that won't turn to mush.

In a medium bowl, toss together the cheese and cornstarch. Set aside.

In a petite French oven, melt the butter over medium heat. Add the shallots and cook for 30 seconds, or until soft and translucent. Add 1 cup wine and mustard. Reduce the heat to low and slowly add a small handful of cheese at a time, stirring well after each addition, until melted and smooth. Whisk in the remaining ¼ cup wine if needed to smooth out the fondue. Stir in the lemon juice, nutmeg, and a large pinch each of salt and pepper.

Transfer the mixture to a fondue pot and serve immediately with bread, apple slices, and vegetables for dipping.

TOASTY HONEY CORN LOAF

FROM MATT LEWIS AND RENATO POLIAFITO OF BAKED

3 large eggs, at room temperature

1½ cups buttermilk, at room temperature

¼ cup plus 2 tablespoons honey, plus more for serving

6 tablespoons unsalted butter, melted and cooled

1¾ cups plus 2 tablespoons yellow cornmeal

1 cup plus 2 tablespoons all-purpose flour

1½ tablespoons baking powder

¼ cup plus 2 tablespoons firmly packed light brown sugar

3 tablespoons granulated sugar

1½ teaspoons kosher salt

2 tablespoons unsalted butter, plus more for serving

There are two schools of thought when it comes to cornbread: sweet or savory. This one is for those who fall solidly into the sweet camp, not surprising considering it comes from Matt Lewis and Renato Poliafito, the gentlemen bakers behind New York City's Baked. Don't worry, this corn loaf is still more bread than cake, with its tang of buttermilk and the soft mellowness of honey. Topped with a pat of melted butter and a drizzle of honey, it is cornbread perfection. Consider serving slices with Brunswick Stew (page 120).

Preheat the oven to 400°F. Place a cast-iron loaf pan in the oven while the oven is preheating.

In a medium bowl, lightly whisk the eggs. Add the buttermilk, honey, and melted butter and whisk until combined. Set aside.

In a large bowl, whisk the cornmeal, flour, baking powder, both sugars, and salt. Make a well in the middle of the dry ingredients, pour the wet ingredients into the well, and gently fold until just combined.

Carefully remove the hot loaf pan from the oven. Drop about 2 tablespoons butter into the pan and swirl to coat the bottom, then use a pastry brush to coat the sides of the pan. Pour the batter into the pan and bake for 25 to 35 minutes, until the top is golden brown and a toothpick inserted into the center of the loaf comes out clean. Let cool on a wire rack for about 10 minutes before popping the loaf out of the pan. Slice and serve while warm with a slather of butter and a drizzle of honey.

GRILLED FLATBREAD

MAKES 2 FLATBREADS

1¼ cups lukewarm water
(95°F to 100°F)

1½ teaspoons active dry yeast

3 cups all-purpose flour

1 teaspoon salt

1 tablespoon olive oil

TOPPINGS

Dried herbs

Olive oil

Grated Parmesan cheese

Flaky sea salt

Grilling pizza dough on the stovetop creates a flatbread that's charred on the outside and chewy on the inside thanks to cast iron's ability to evenly retain high heat. A classic way to finish the flatbread is with olive oil and flaky sea salt. Or feel free to add whichever toppings you fancy; dried herbs, flavored olive oil, and even grated Parmesan cheese would all be perfect.

Pour the lukewarm water into a small bowl and add the yeast. Let the yeast proof for about 5 minutes, until bubbly.

In the bowl of a food processor fitted with the dough blade, combine the flour, salt, and olive oil. With the motor running, drizzle in the yeast mixture through the feed tube and pulse until the dough comes together in a ball.

Coat a medium bowl with olive oil and place the dough in the bowl, turning to coat the dough in the oil. Cover with plastic wrap and let the dough proof in a warm spot for 2 to 3 hours, or in the refrigerator overnight, until doubled in size. (Take the dough out of the refrigerator 30 minutes before rolling it out to come to room temperature.)

Preheat a cast-iron grill pan over medium-high heat. Divide the dough in half and roll each half into a 10-inch oval on a lightly floured surface. Brush each side of the dough with oil. Place one round on the grill pan and cook for 4 to 5 minutes per side, or until golden brown and grill marks are present. Repeat with the remaining dough, top with your choice of toppings, slice, and serve.

GARLIC AND HERB PARKER HOUSE ROLLS

MAKES 18 ROLLS

¾ cup unsalted butter

1¼ cups whole milk

3 tablespoons sugar

1 (¼-ounce) envelope
(2¼ teaspoons) active
dry yeast

4 to 4¼ cups
all-purpose flour

1 large egg

2 tablespoons chopped fresh
herbs, such as rosemary
and thyme

4 cloves garlic, minced

2 teaspoons kosher salt

Flaky sea salt

There's nothing more inviting at the table than warm, soft Parker House rolls. This version is flavored with herbs and garlic.

In a petite French oven, melt ½ cup of the butter over medium heat. Add the milk and sugar and stir to combine. Using a thermometer, check the temperature of the butter and milk mixture; when it's 105°F, remove it from the heat. Add the yeast and stir to dissolve. Let the yeast bloom for about 5 minutes, until the mixture is bubbly. If mixture does not bubble and smell "yeasty," throw it out and start over.

Pour the yeast mixture into the bowl of a stand mixer fitted with a dough hook. Add 4 cups of flour. Turn the mixer to low and knead until just combined, about 1 minute. Add the egg, 1½ tablespoons of the chopped herbs, half of the garlic, and the kosher salt, and continue kneading on low speed until soft and smooth, tacky but not sticky, adding the remaining ¼ cup flour if the dough is too wet.

On a lightly floured surface, shape the dough into a ball and place it in a large greased bowl. Cover with plastic wrap and let dough rise in a warm, draft-free area for about 1½ hours, until doubled in size.

Remove the plastic wrap and gently punch down the dough. Cut the dough into 4 equal pieces, then shape into small balls about 2 ounces each for 18 dough balls in total.

Butter a large cast-iron roasting pan and place the shaped dough into the dish. Let the dough rise for 30 minutes. While the dough is rising, preheat the oven to 350°F.

Bake the rolls for 25 to 30 minutes, until golden brown.

In a small cast-iron fry pan, melt the remaining ¼ cup butter with the remaining garlic. Gently brush the dough with the melted garlic butter, top with the remaining herbs, and sprinkle with sea salt. Serve warm.

NO-KNEAD CAST-IRON BREAD

MAKES I LOAF

3 cups bread flour, plus more for the work surface

2 teaspoons salt

¼ teaspoon active dry yeast

1⅓ cups lukewarm water, plus more as needed

The combination of flour, salt, yeast, and water is a magical one, producing a variety of loaves that grace dinner tables around the world. Still, there is something extra special in this no-knead bread, inspired by the original recipe by Jim Lahey, the bread maestro behind New York City's Sullivan Street Bakery. Even the most intimidated bread baker can feel confident using Lahey's method, which requires little work but a bit of time. Here the rise time is slightly increased, with an easier way to get the sticky dough into a hot cocotte, the ideal bread-baking vessel because its steam creates a crispy crust.

In a large bowl, combine the flour, salt, and yeast. Pour in the lukewarm water and, using a wooden spoon, stir the mixture until it comes together into a sticky dough. If it isn't sticky, add more water, a couple tablespoons at a time, to get there. Cover with a clean kitchen towel and keep in a draft-free place for 18 to 24 hours.

Lightly flour a work surface. Gently remove the dough from the bowl onto the work surface. Form the dough into a ball, gently tucking the sides of the dough under. Place the dough onto a large piece of parchment paper. Cover with a clean kitchen towel and let the dough rise for 1 to 2 hours, until doubled in size.

Preheat the oven to 475°F. Place a medium cast-iron cocotte into the oven while it preheats.

When the cocotte is hot, carefully remove it from the oven. Using the parchment paper sides as handles, gently lower the dough into the cocotte. Cover the cocotte, place it into the oven, and bake for 30 minutes. Remove the lid and continue baking for another 20 to 30 minutes, until the bread is golden brown in color. Remove the bread from the cocotte and allow to cool for 1 hour before slicing and serving.

BROCCOLI RABE PIZZA WITH CARAMELIZED ONIONS AND BURRATA

MAKES TWO 10-INCH PIZZAS

DOUGH

1½ teaspoons active dry yeast

1¼ cups lukewarm water

3 cups flour

1 teaspoon salt

1 tablespoon extra-virgin olive oil, plus more for bowl

TOPPING

6 tablespoons olive oil, plus more for garnish

3 onions, thinly sliced

12 ounces broccoli rabe, ends trimmed

2 cloves garlic, minced

¼ teaspoon red chili flakes, plus more for garnish

Kosher salt

8 ounces burrata cheese, torn into 2-inch pieces

Flaky sea salt, to taste

If you don't have an outdoor pizza oven, a cast-iron pan is the next best thing for capturing that elusive crispy and chewy crust. This pizza dough can be made the day before and proofed overnight in the refrigerator. If you use this method, just make sure you let the dough come to room temperature for at least 30 minutes before cooking.

Broccoli rabe, also known as rapini, is a cruciferous vegetable with a pleasantly bitter taste. Blanching the broccoli rabe mellows out the bitterness and adds a wonderful texture and flavor to the pizza. This pizza can also be prepped ahead by caramelizing the onions up to 3 days before and blanching the broccoli rabe the day before.

To make the dough: Add the yeast and water to a small bowl. Let yeast proof for about 5 minutes or until bubbly.

In the bowl of a food processor fitted with a dough blade, add the flour, salt, and 1 tablespoon olive oil. With the motor running, drizzle in the yeast mixture. Pulse until dough comes together in a ball.

Add the remaining olive oil to a medium bowl. Place the dough in the bowl, coating the dough with the olive oil. Cover with plastic wrap and let dough proof for about 2 to 3 hours at room temperature, until puffy. You may also proof the dough in the refrigerator overnight.

While the dough is proofing, make the topping: Caramelize the onions by placing a fry pan over medium-low heat. Add 2 tablespoons of olive oil and the onions. Cook the onions for about 30 minutes, stirring occasionally until the onions are golden brown, adding a couple tablespoons of water at a time if the pan gets dry. Remove from heat and set aside.

continued

Preheat oven to 450°F.

Bring a large pot of water to boil and blanch the broccoli rabe for about 1 minute, or until the broccoli rabe turns bright green. Carefully remove from the water and place in an ice bath. Once the broccoli rabe is cool, remove and let dry on a paper towel. Roughly chop into 2-inch pieces.

In the same fry pan used for the onions, add 2 tablespoons olive oil over medium heat. Add the garlic and red pepper flakes and sauté for about 30 seconds. Add the broccoli rabe and large pinch of salt, and sauté for another 3 to 5 minutes or until the broccoli rabe is just tender. Remove from the pan and set aside.

Assemble the pizza by dividing the dough into two. Roll out the dough into a 10-inch round. Place the dough into a cold 10-inch cast-iron fry pan. Cook the pizza dough over medium heat on the stovetop until the bottom of the pizza dough is set, about 1 to 2 minutes. Brush the entire pizza with 1 tablespoon olive oil then top with half of the onions and half of the broccoli rabe.

Place the pizza in the oven and bake for 6 to 8 minutes, or until crust is golden brown. Carefully remove the pizza from the oven and top with half of the burrata. Return pizza to the oven and bake for another 5 to 7 minutes, or until the burrata is melted and the crust is golden brown.

Drizzle with olive oil, a pinch of flaky sea salt, and red pepper flakes. Repeat with remaining ingredients for remaining pizza.

Serve immediately.

GRILLED CHEESE WITH FIG PRESERVES, SAGE, PROSCIUTTO, AND BRIE

MAKES 2 SERVINGS

4 slices hearty bread, such as sourdough or ciabatta

2 tablespoons olive oil

¼ cup fig preserves

4 ounces Brie cheese, rinds removed

1 tablespoon chopped fresh sage

4 slices prosciutto

Grilled cheese is one of life's simpler pleasures, but that doesn't mean it can't be improved upon. This updated version is made with luscious Brie, salty prosciutto, and the grounding sweetness of figs. Make sure to choose a sturdy, crusty bread, such as a sourdough or ciabatta, that can stand up to grilling. A cast-iron pan will help you get a golden brown crust that tastes as good as it looks. This gourmet grilled cheese can be cut into wedges for hors d'oeuvres or accompanied by a salad for an effortless dinner.

Preheat a medium cast-iron fry pan over medium-high heat.

Brush slices of bread with olive oil on both sides. Lay 2 of the bread slices on a cutting board. Spread half of the jam on one slice of bread. Top with half of the Brie and the half of the sage. Top with another slice of bread. Repeat with the remaining ingredients to make a second sandwich.

Grill 1 sandwich on both sides until the cheese is melted and the jam is warmed through. Carefully open the sandwich and place the prosciutto into the grilled cheese. Repeat with the second sandwich. Cut the sandwiches in half and serve immediately.

BROWN RICE BOWL WITH ARUGULA PESTO, PRESERVED LEMON, AND ROASTED BEETS

MAKES 2 TO 4 SERVINGS

½ cup white wine vinegar

I tablespoon sugar

I½ teaspoons salt

I bunch radishes, thinly sliced

I bunch beets,
greens removed

I cup brown rice, rinsed

½ cup walnuts

I clove garlic, minced

¼ cup Parmesan cheese

2 cups packed arugula

Kosher salt

Freshly ground black pepper

I cup olive oil

I tablespoon preserved
lemon, diced

I avocado, pit removed
and diced

¼ cup feta, crumbled

Walnut oil, for drizzling
(optional)

Flaky sea salt

Technically this dish doesn't have to be served in a bowl; however, when you pile on all the delicious toppings, it might just be the easiest way to eat it.

In this recipe, brown rice is flavored with a nutty and spicy arugula pesto, then topped with roasted beets, pickled radish, and avocado. The end result is a hearty but really healthy dish that is great for lunch or dinner. If you can't find preserved lemon, just substitute a squeeze of fresh lemon juice. The walnut-oil drizzle is completely optional but adds another layer of nuttiness to the dish and pairs perfectly with the roasted beets.

In a petite French oven, bring the vinegar, 1 cup of water, sugar, and salt to a boil. Remove from heat and add radish slices to the pot. Let the mixture sit at room temperature for 1 hour.

Preheat the oven to 350°F.

Place the beets in a shallow, medium cast-iron roasting pan. Cover halfway with water, then cover the entire pan with aluminum foil.

Place the beets in the oven and roast for 50 to 60 minutes, until fork-tender. Remove and let cool. When cool to the touch, remove the skin and cut into bite-size pieces.

While the beets cook, make the rice by placing it in a petite French oven. Add 2 cups water and bring to a boil. Reduce the heat to low, cover, and cook rice for 40 to 45 minutes, until all the water is absorbed. Remove from the heat and let the rice stand for 10 minutes, covered, then fluff with a fork. Set aside.

Make the pesto by combining the walnuts, garlic, Parmesan cheese, arugula, and a large pinch each of kosher salt and pepper in the bowl of a food processor. Pulse to combine. With the motor running, drizzle in the olive oil. Taste for salt and pepper.

Assemble the bowl by tossing ½ cup pesto with the rice. Save the remaining pesto for another use. Fold the preserved lemon into the rice.

Divide the rice among individual bowls. Top each rice bowl with a handful of beets, avocado, feta cheese, pickled radishes and a drizzle of walnut oil. Sprinkle with flaky sea salt and serve.

SUMMERTIME PASTA WITH TOMATOES AND CHARRED CORN

MAKES 2 TO 4 SERVINGS

Salt

8 ounces angel hair pasta

2 ears corn, kernels removed from the cob

2 tablespoons olive oil

I pint cherry tomatoes

I large shallot, minced

2 cloves garlic, minced

½ cup chicken stock

2 tablespoons fresh lemon juice

2 tablespoons unsalted butter

¼ cup crumbled ricotta salata or grated Parmesan cheese

¼ cup chopped fresh herbs, such as basil or thyme

Freshly ground black pepper

This light and fresh pasta dish is bursting with summer's seasonal favorites. Cherry tomatoes are blistered and corn is charred in a cast-iron pan for an effortless sauce that captures fresh-off-the-grill flavor without the need for an outdoor grill. If you don't have angel hair pasta, you can use any dried pasta you have in your cabinet. Serve al fresco on the deck or at a summer picnic with a chilled rosé.

When you char the corn in the cast-iron fry pan, inevitably it will leave some black charred pieces of corn in the pan. If you only use one pan for the recipe, don't be alarmed at the occasional black fleck in your pasta, or feel free to char the corn in the pan and either use another pan for the tomato sauce or carefully clean the hot pan before moving onto the next steps in the recipe.

Bring a large cast-iron cocotte of water to a boil, salt it, and cook the pasta according to the package instructions to al dente. Drain, reserving ½ cup of the cooking liquid, and set aside.

In a large cast-iron fry pan, add the corn kernels over medium-high heat and sauté kernels for 3 to 5 minutes, stirring occasionally until corn is lightly charred. Remove the corn to a bowl and and cover to keep it warm. Heat the oil in the pan, then add the tomatoes and cook until they are blistered and slightly wilted, 3 to 5 minutes. Add the shallot and garlic and cook for about 30 seconds. Add the chicken stock and lemon juice and cook for 2 to 3 minutes, until the liquid is slightly reduced. Fold in the butter, pasta, corn, and some or all of the reserved pasta water as needed to loosen the sauce. Top with the ricotta salata, fresh herbs, and a large pinch of salt and pepper, and serve.

OVEN-BAKED RISOTTO WITH LEMON, ASPARAGUS, AND EGG YOLK

MAKES 6 TO 8 SERVINGS

1 tablespoon olive oil

1 onion, diced

2 cloves garlic, minced

1½ cups arborio rice

½ cup white wine

4½ cups chicken or vegetable stock

2 teaspoons lemon zest

Salt and freshly ground black pepper

2 cups (1-inch spears) asparagus, blanched

1 egg yolk, whisked

¼ cup grated Parmesan cheese

Chopped fresh flat-leaf parsley, for garnish

Chopped chives, for garnish

There's no need to stand at your stove stirring to be rewarded with a successful risotto. Baking your risotto in the oven will give you equally creamy results. An egg yolk folded in just before serving furthers the creamy effect. You may swap out the asparagus for another vegetable such as peas, or add a protein such as shrimp, scallops, or shredded chicken, if you like. Serve as a savory side dish or as a main alongside Grilled Romaine with Lemon and Parmesan (page 28).

Preheat the oven to 350°F.

In a medium cast-iron cocotte, heat the oil over medium-high heat. Add the onion and cook for 2 to 4 minutes, until translucent. Add the garlic and rice and cook for another minute, or until the rice is coated with the oil and the garlic is fragrant. Stir in the wine, 4 cups of the stock, the lemon zest, and big pinch of salt and pepper. Cover and bake for 45 to 50 minutes, until most of the stock is absorbed.

Carefully remove the lid and fold in the blanched asparagus. Cover again and let the asparagus steam for 1 minute to warm it. Add egg yolk, the remaining ½ cup stock, and the cheese, and stir well. Taste and add salt and pepper, if needed. Spoon into bowls and serve garnished with parsley and chives.

TRIPLE CRÈME MAC AND CHEESE

Salt

1 pound pasta, such as fusilli or farfalle

¼ cup unsalted butter

¼ cup all-purpose flour

3 cups milk

¼ teaspoon freshly grated nutmeg

¼ teaspoon freshly ground black pepper

4 ounces triple crème cheese, rind removed and cubed

12 ounces Gruyère cheese, grated

1 teaspoon chopped fresh thyme, plus more for garnish

¼ cup grated Parmesan cheese

¼ cup panko bread crumbs

2 tablespoons olive oil

Triple crème cheese is a creamy, soft, and buttery cow's milk cheese, oozing with over 75 percent butterfat due to the extra cream component. Adding it to mac and cheese puts a French spin on the American classic, increasing its comforting appeal while infusing it with a bit of decadence. Serve this at the holidays or as a Friday night dinner treat, paired with a salad and sparkly Syrah to temper its richness. If you can't find a triple crème cheese, swap in grated sharp white cheddar.

Preheat the oven to 375°F.

Bring a large cast-iron cocotte of water to a boil, salt it, and cook the pasta according to the package instructions for al dente. Drain.

In a large cast-iron cocotte, melt the butter over medium heat. Add the flour and whisk until combined. Cook for 30 seconds, whisking constantly until a smooth paste forms. Add the milk and whisk until smooth. Bring to a boil, then reduce the heat and cook for 3 to 5 minutes, until the mixture thickens and coats the back of a spoon. Add the nutmeg, pepper, triple crème and Gruyère cheeses, and thyme. Season with salt. Fold in the cooked pasta. Keep the mixture in the large cocotte for baking, or split it among 6 to 8 mini cocottes for individual portions.

In a small bowl, combine the Parmesan cheese, panko, and oil. Top the mac and cheese with the Parmesan mixture, place in the oven, and bake for 20 to 30 minutes for the large cocotte or 20 to 25 minutes for the minis, until the top is golden brown and bubbling. Serve hot.

ONE-PAN WILD MUSHROOM LASAGNA

2 tablespoons olive oil

2 pounds wild mushrooms, sliced

Salt

I large shallot, minced

¼ cup unsalted butter

¼ cup all-purpose flour

3 cups milk

Pinch of freshly grated nutmeg

Freshly ground black pepper

2 cups whole-milk ricotta

2 large eggs

I tablespoon chopped fresh thyme, plus more for garnish

2 cups shredded Gruyère cheese

2½ cups shredded mozzarella cheese

12 ounces no-cook lasagna noodles

Parmesan cheese, for finishing

This standout vegetarian lasagna is layered with mushrooms and cheese and blanketed in a simple white sauce. The lasagna is made in a single cast-iron fry pan, making cleanup super easy.

In a 12-inch cast-iron fry pan, heat the oil over medium-high heat. Working in batches, add the mushrooms and a large pinch of salt and cook until golden brown, 2 to 4 minutes. Remove to a bowl and set aside.

Add the shallot to the same pan and cook over medium heat for 30 seconds. Add the butter and stir until melted. Add the flour and cook, stirring, for 1 to 2 minutes, until the flour turns light brown in color. Slowly whisk in the milk and cook, whisking, until thickened, 3 to 4 minutes, taking care not to let the sauce reduce too much. Add the nutmeg and a large pinch each of salt and pepper. Pour the béchamel into a medium bowl and set aside.

In a small bowl, combine the ricotta, eggs, thyme, and a pinch each of salt and pepper. In a separate bowl, combine the Gruyère and mozzarella.

Assemble the lasagna by spreading a quarter of the béchamel on the bottom of the fry pan. Top with a quarter of the lasagna noodles, then spoon on a quarter of the ricotta mixture, a quarter of the mushrooms, and a handful of the Gruyère-mozzarella cheese mixture. Repeat two more times, ending with the noodles on top. Spread the remaining béchamel, mushrooms, and cheese mixture over the top. Top with a sprinkle of salt, pepper, and thyme leaves.

Cover with aluminum foil and bake for 30 to 40 minutes, then uncover and continue to bake until bubbling and golden brown on top, 8 to 10 minutes. Let lasagna rest for about 10 minutes, then slice and serve with Parmesan cheese.

THREE CHEESE AND SPINACH STUFFED SHELLS

MAKES 4 TO 6 SERVINGS

15 ounces whole milk ricotta cheese

1 cup grated Parmesan cheese

1 large egg

¼ cup chopped fresh basil

2 tablespoons chopped fresh flat-leaf parsley, plus more for garnish

Pinch of freshly grated nutmeg

2 cups grated mozzarella cheese

Salt

Red pepper flakes

8 ounces jumbo pasta shells

3 tablespoons olive oil

5 ounces fresh spinach leaves

1 onion, diced

3 cloves garlic, minced

1 (28-ounce) can crushed tomatoes, with juices

2 teaspoons Worcestershire sauce

This pasta is perfect for an easy Sunday night dinner. The homemade tomato sauce is flavored with a secret ingredient—Worcestershire sauce—for a tasty umami note.

In a large bowl, combine the ricotta cheese, ½ cup of Parmesan cheese, the egg, basil, parsley, nutmeg, 1 cup of the mozzarella cheese, and a large pinch of salt and red pepper flakes. Stir well and set aside.

Cook the pasta shells in a large cast-iron cocotte of boiling salted water according to the package instructions for al dente. Drain and set aside to cool.

In a rectangular cast-iron roasting or fry pan, heat 1 tablespoon of the oil over medium heat. Add the spinach and cook until wilted. Remove the spinach and place it on a paper towel–lined plate. Carefully squeeze the excess liquid out of the spinach and fold the spinach into the ricotta cheese mixture.

In the same cast-iron pan, heat the remaining 2 tablespoons oil over medium heat. Add the onion and cook for 3 to 5 minutes, until softened. Add the garlic and cook for another 30 seconds. Add the tomatoes and Worcestershire sauce and cook for 5 minutes, or until the sauce is reduced and thickened slightly. Taste and add more salt if needed. Carefully pour half of the sauce into a bowl and set aside.

Assemble the stuffed shells by spreading the remaining pasta sauce across the bottom of the roasting pan. Stuff the cooked pasta shells with the cheese filling and place the shells open-side up in the roasting pan. Pour the reserved sauce over the shells and top with the remaining 1 cup mozzarella cheese and ½ cup Parmesan cheese.

Cover with aluminum foil and bake for 25 minutes. Remove the foil and bake until the cheese is golden brown, about 10 minutes more. Remove from the oven and serve piping hot, garnished with parsley.

GINGERY VIETNAMESE CHICKEN WITH NOODLES

CHICKEN

1 cup coconut milk

2 cloves garlic, minced

2 tablespoons fish sauce

2 tablespoons soy sauce

2 tablespoons honey

2 tablespoons vegetable oil

1 stalk (about 4 inches) lemongrass, white parts only, thinly sliced

1 tablespoon grated peeled fresh ginger

1½ pounds boneless, skinless chicken thighs, cut into 1-inch pieces

DIPPING SAUCE

1 Thai bird chile, or ½ serrano chile

2 cloves garlic, minced

3 tablespoons sugar

½ cup boiling water

Juice of 2 limes

5 tablespoons fish sauce

Cooked rice noodles

Cucumber slices

Beet sprouts

Carrots, julienned

Mint leaves

Peanuts

This might seem like an ordinary noodle bowl, but it is anything but. The chicken is marinated in spices and coconut milk so that it stays extra juicy when hit with the heat of the grill pan. The chicken is tossed with noodles and fresh herbs, then drizzled with the sweet, sour, and savory traditional Vietnamese dipping sauce, *nuoc cham*. If you don't care for fish sauce, you can subsitute additional soy sauce, but fish sauce will give the most authentic flavor. With its bright citrus, ginger, and chiles, this noodle dish will pep up your palate year-round.

Marinate the chicken: In a medium bowl, combine the coconut milk, garlic, fish sauce, soy sauce, honey, oil, lemongrass, and ginger. Add the chicken, cover, and marinate in the refrigerator for at least 3 hours or overnight.

Make the dipping sauce: In a small bowl, combine the chile, garlic, and sugar. With the back of a spoon, smash the ingredients together, forming a rough paste. Add the boiling water, lime juice, and fish sauce. Stir well and let cool in the refrigerator.

When you are ready to serve, soak 4 to 6 wooden skewers in water to cover for 15 minutes.

Preheat a cast-iron grill pan over medium-high heat.

Thread the chicken onto the skewers and grill for 12 to 14 minutes, turning halfway through, until the internal temperature reaches 165°F. Remove the chicken from the grill pan to a platter and let rest for 5 minutes. Have your guests arrange the noodles, cucumber, sprouts, carrots, mint, and peanuts on their plates. Drizzle the chicken with the dipping sauce and serve any extra sauce alongside.

ONE-POT ORECCHIETTE WITH SWISS CHARD, SAUSAGE, AND LEMON

MAKES 4 TO 6 SERVINGS

Salt

1 pound dried orecchiette pasta

2 tablespoons olive oil

1 pound pork sausage, casings removed

¾ pound Swiss chard, stems removed, roughly chopped

¼ cup chicken stock

½ cup grated Parmesan cheese

1 teaspoon lemon zest

Pinch of red pepper flakes

This easy weeknight dinner is hearty and comes together in minutes, plus it's super easy to clean up. The Italian sausage provides a flavorful base, and orecchiette, traditionally made with semolina flour, has an addictively toothsome bite. Orecchiette means "little ears" in Italian, and its cuplike shape splendidly holds flavors together. If you can't find orecchiette, you can easily try another type of shaped pasta, like farfalle. Feel free to use this recipe as a template, substituting turkey or chicken sausage and kale or mustard greens.

Bring a large cast-iron cocotte of water to a boil, salt it, and cook the orecchiette according to the package instructions to al dente. Drain and set aside.

In a large cast-iron cocotte, heat the oil over medium heat. Add the sausage and cook until cooked through and browned, 5 to 7 minutes, breaking up large pieces of meat. Add the chard and chicken stock, cover, and cook for 2 to 3 minutes, until the chard is wilted.

Uncover and fold in the pasta. Heat briefly to allow some excess liquid to evaporate, then fold in the cheese and lemon zest. Season with salt, add the red pepper flakes, and serve immediately.

PORK RAGÙ WITH PAPPARDELLE

2 pounds boneless pork shoulder, cut into 2-inch cubes

Salt and freshly ground black pepper

2 tablespoons vegetable oil

I onion, diced

2 carrots, diced

2 celery stalks, diced

I bulb fennel, cored and thinly sliced

I teaspoon fennel seeds

2 teaspoons chopped fresh sage

2 cloves garlic, minced

I cup red wine

I (28-ounce) can crushed tomatoes

2 cups chicken stock

12 ounces fresh pappardelle

Parmesan cheese, for garnish

Ragù is most often made with beef, but here tender pork shoulder creates a luscious and delicious sauce to toss with pasta. Use fresh pappardelle if you can find it, but if you can't, dried pappardelle, spaghetti, or linguine will work just fine. This ragù gets better the longer it sits, so if you have the time, consider making it a day ahead. Serve with the Grilled Romaine with Lemon and Parmesan (page 28) and a hearty Italian red wine, like Barolo.

Preheat oven to 350°F.

Sprinkle the pork shoulder with salt and pepper.

In a large cast-iron cocotte, heat the oil over medium-high heat. Brown the pork on all sides, 6 to 8 minutes, working in batches if needed, removing the pork to a bowl as it is browned. Carefully remove all but 2 tablespoons fat from the pan. Add the onion, carrots, celery, fennel, and a big pinch of salt and pepper. Cook for 4 to 6 minutes, until softened.

Add the fennel seeds, sage, and garlic and cook for 30 seconds. Deglaze the cocotte with the wine, then add the tomatoes and chicken stock. Return the pork to the cocotte, bring to a simmer, then reduce the heat to low, cover, and braise in the oven for 2½ hours, or until the pork is fork-tender. Remove the lid and cook for another 30 minutes, or until the sauce is reduced slightly.

Meanwhile, bring a large cocotte of water to a boil, salt it, and cook the pappardelle according to the package instructions for al dente. Drain.

Remove the pork from the braising liquid and shred it with two forks. Return the pork to the cocotte, taste, and add more salt and pepper if needed. Toss the pasta with the pork ragù and serve immediately, topped with cheese.

SOUPS & STEWS

Smoky Corn Chowder
with Bacon Croutons 107

Miso Pumpkin Soup with Walnut
and Sesame Seed Brittle 108

Sungold Tomato Gazpacho with
Cucumber, Avocado, and Burrata 111

Classic Roasted Tomato Soup 112

Kale, Quinoa, and Butternut
Squash Stew 113

Coq au Vin Blanc 114

Chicken Meatballs in Red
Coconut Curry Sauce 117

Dungeness Crab Stew
with Fennel and Citrus 118

Brunswick Stew 120

Lamb Stew with Turkish Beans
and Pickled Tomatoes 121

Beer-Braised Short Ribs 122

Beef Bourguignon 125

SMOKY CORN CHOWDER WITH BACON CROUTONS

MAKES 4 TO 6 SERVINGS

4 ounces bacon, cut into ½-inch cubes

I onion, diced

2 russet potatoes (about 1½ pounds), peeled and diced

6 ears corn, husks removed, kernels removed from the cob, and cobs cut in half crosswise

1½ teaspoons smoked paprika

½ teaspoon ground cumin

Kosher salt

Chopped fresh cilantro, for garnish

Freshly ground black pepper

Flaky sea salt

Dairy-free, yet full of flavor, this recipe has a Southwestern kick, spiced with smoked paprika, cumin, and sprinkled with cilantro. It's a common misconception that a lot of cream is required to give soup a soft, silky texture. Another way is to cook vegetables until they are almost falling apart and then blending them into a creamy base. This is how we craft our chowder, going one easy step further with a corn-cob stock that intensifies flavor while acting as a natural thickener.

In a large cast-iron cocotte, cook the bacon over medium heat until crispy and the fat is rendered, 3 to 5 minutes. Remove the bacon to a paper towel–lined plate. Add the onion and potatoes to the pan and cook for 35 to 45 minutes, until the vegetables are very soft and almost falling apart.

While the onion and potatoes are cooking, place the corn cobs in a separate cocotte and add water to cover. Bring to a simmer over high heat, then reduce the heat to low and cook for 35 to 45 minutes, or until the stock is opaque, adding more water if necessary to keep the corn cobs covered. Remove the cobs from the stock. Add some of the stock to the onions and potatoes as they cook if the pan starts to get dry.

Add all but ¼ cup of the corn kernels, the smoked paprika, cumin, a large pinch of kosher salt, and 2 cups of the corn-cob stock to the onion and potatoes. Bring to a simmer, then reduce the heat to medium-low and cook for 5 minutes. Transfer to a blender and add another 2 cups of the corn-cob stock. Blend on high speed until smooth and silky (be careful blending hot liquids), adding more stock or water if the soup is too thick. Freeze extra stock in freezer safe plastic container.

Divide the soup among bowls and top with the reserved fresh corn, the bacon, some cilantro, pepper, and a pinch of flaky sea salt.

MISO PUMPKIN SOUP WITH WALNUT AND SESAME SEED BRITTLE

MAKES 6 TO 8 SERVINGS

BRITTLE

I cup sugar

I tablespoon lemon juice

2 tablespoons unsalted butter

½ cup chopped toasted walnuts

½ cup black sesame seeds

Flaky sea salt

SOUP

3½ pounds pumpkin, such as sugar pie pumpkin, cut in half and seeded

4 tablespoons olive oil

I onion, diced

I pound sweet potatoes, peeled and diced

2 cloves garlic, peeled

Salt and freshly ground black pepper

Pinch of freshly grated nutmeg

2 tablespoons white or yellow miso

I quart vegetable stock

I tablespoon sherry vinegar

Crème fraîche (optional)

Great homemade pumpkin soup starts with freshly roasted pumpkin. This one is gussied up with sweet potatoes, added for depth and sweetness, and miso, which imparts an earthy umami note. This soup is excellent on its own, but what sets it apart is the brittle. Its salty-sweet flavor and crunchy texture are a great foil for the silky soup.

Make the brittle: Line a baking sheet with parchment paper. Combine the sugar, lemon juice, and ½ cup water in a petite French oven. Heat over medium-low heat, stirring occasionally, until the sugar is dissolved. Continue cooking until the liquid turns amber in color, 5 to 7 minutes. Add the butter and stir well. Fold in the walnuts and sesame seeds. Carefully pour the brittle onto the prepared baking sheet, sprinkle with salt, and let cool for 1 hour. Carefully chop the brittle into small bite-size pieces.

Meanwhile, make the soup: Preheat the oven to 425°F and line a baking sheet with parchment paper.

Brush the pumpkin with 2 tablespoons of the oil and lay it flesh-side down on the prepared baking sheet. Roast for 30 to 40 minutes, until softened. Set aside to cool slightly.

Heat the remaining 2 tablespoons oil in a large cast-iron cocotte over medium heat. Add the onion and sweet potatoes and cook for 10 to 12 minutes, until the sweet potatoes are softened. Add the garlic, a large pinch each of salt and pepper, and the nutmeg and cook for another 30 seconds. Scoop in chunks of the cooked pumpkin and cook for another 5 minutes. Add the miso and stock and stir well to combine. Bring to a boil, then reduce the heat to maintain a simmer for 5 minutes.

Working in batches, blend the soup until smooth and return to the cocotte. Spoon into bowls and serve immediately, with a dollop of crème fraîche, and a sprinkle of brittle.

SUNGOLD TOMATO GAZPACHO WITH CUCUMBER, AVOCADO, AND BURRATA

MAKES 4 TO 6 SERVINGS

GAZPACHO

2¼ pounds ripe Sungold tomatoes

1 medium or 2 small green bell peppers, roughly chopped

1 cucumber, about 8 inches long, peeled, seeded, and roughly chopped

½ red onion, roughly chopped

2 cloves garlic

4 to 6 tablespoons sherry vinegar

1 tablespoon fresh lemon juice

¼ teaspoon smoked paprika

Kosher salt

¼ cup olive oil, plus more for drizzling

TOPPINGS

½ firm but ripe avocado, diced

½ cucumber, peeled and diced

2 tablespoons minced red onion

Fresh burrata cheese

Olive oil

Snipped fresh chives

Flaky sea salt

Freshly ground black pepper

When the heat of summer is on full blast, few dishes are more refreshing than gazpacho. This recipe uses Sungold tomatoes, an incredibly sweet type of cherry tomato with a beautiful golden hue. If you can't find Sungolds, swap in whatever cherry tomatoes look best at your market. Sherry vinegar balances the sweetness of the tomatoes; make sure to taste your soup and add more as needed. And don't skip the flaky finishing salt—tomatoes love salt. Pair the gazpacho with proscuitto sandwiches for a cool summer meal that avoids the hot stove.

Make the gazpacho: In a blender, combine the tomatoes, green bell pepper, cucumber, red onion, garlic, 4 tablespoons vinegar, the lemon juice, paprika, oil, and a large pinch of kosher salt. Blend until smooth, adding water as needed if the soup is too thick. Taste and add more salt and/or vinegar as needed to balance the sweetness of the tomatoes. Place in a cast-iron cocotte (we love the tomato cocotte for this recipe) and refrigerate the soup for about 1 hour or until well chilled.

In a medium bowl, combine the avocado, cucumber, and red onion. Pour the soup into soup bowls and top each with some of the avocado mixture. Add a dollop of burrata, a drizzle of oil, some chives, and a sprinkling of flaky sea salt and black pepper.

CLASSIC ROASTED TOMATO SOUP

2 (28-ounce) cans whole San Marzano tomatoes

4 cloves garlic

4 sprigs thyme

1 teaspoon salt

Pinch of red pepper flakes

3 tablespoons olive oil

1 onion, diced

2 tablespoons tomato paste

2 teaspoons soy sauce

2 cups chicken or vegetable stock

It's hard to beat a comforting bowl of tomato soup on a cold night or when you're feeling a little under the weather. Thanks to canned tomatoes, you can make this recipe all year-round. If you haven't already done so, try San Marzano tomatoes. They are processed at the height of the season and are often more flavorful than fresh tomatoes, especially in the winter. In this recipe, the tomatoes are roasted to intensify their bright notes, and tomato paste and soy sauce are added to amp up the intensity.

Make sure to use parchment paper, not aluminum foil, for roasting the tomatoes, because foil will react with the acid in the tomatoes. Consider sprucing up this simple tomato soup by finishing it with toppings such as brown butter croutons, crème fraîche, toasted hazelnuts, crumbled Parmesan wafers, and fresh herbs.

Preheat the oven to 425°F.

Pour the tomatoes, along with their liquid, onto a parchment-lined baking sheet in a single layer. Top with the garlic, thyme, salt, red pepper flakes, and 2 tablespoons of the oil. Roast the tomatoes for 35 to 40 minutes, until they are soft and caramelized. Remove and discard the thyme sprigs and let cool slightly.

While the tomatoes are cooling, in a medium cast-iron cocotte, heat the remaining 1 tablespoon oil over medium heat. Add the onion and cook until softened and translucent, 3 to 5 minutes. Add the tomato paste and cook for 1 minute. Add the soy sauce, stock, and roasted tomato mixture and simmer for about 15 minutes, or until the mixture has slightly reduced.

Transfer to a blender in batches and blend until smooth. Add salt and red pepper flakes to taste. Spoon into bowls and serve.

KALE, QUINOA, AND BUTTERNUT SQUASH STEW

MAKES 4 TO 6 SERVINGS

2 tablespoons olive oil

I onion, diced

I small butternut squash (about 1½ pounds), peeled, cut in half lengthwise, seeds removed, and diced

Salt and freshly ground black pepper

3 cloves garlic, minced

2 teaspoons chili powder

I teaspoon smoked paprika

I (28-ounce) can diced tomatoes, with juices

2 cups vegetable stock

¾ cup white quinoa, rinsed

I bunch kale, stems removed and roughly chopped

Flaky sea salt

Chopped fresh cilantro, for garnish

Hearty one-pot meals that come together in less than an hour are a home cook's bread and butter. If they are super healthy, even better. This recipe is packed with superfoods—iron-rich kale, vitamin A–heavy butternut squash, and quinoa, a complete protein that provides essential amino acids. This nutrient-dense stew is sure to make repeat appearances at your table. It may not be terribly glamorous, but it is nourishing and delicious, perfect for weeknight suppers with family and friends. Feel free to top it with goat or feta cheese if you want to increase the protein.

In a medium cast-iron cocotte, heat the oil over medium heat. Add the onion, squash, and a large pinch each of salt and pepper and cook for 5 to 7 minutes, until the onion is softened. Add the garlic, chili powder, and smoked paprika and cook for 1 minute. Add the tomatoes, vegetable stock, and quinoa. Bring to a boil, then reduce the heat and simmer for about 30 minutes, until the quinoa is cooked through.

Add the kale, cover, and cook for another 5 minutes, or until the kale is wilted. Taste and adjust the seasonings with salt and pepper. Spoon into bowls and serve with sea salt and cilantro.

COQ AU VIN BLANC

MAKES 4 TO 6 SERVINGS

6 ounces bacon, cut into
½-inch pieces

I (3½-pound) chicken,
cut into 10 pieces

Salt and freshly ground
black pepper

I yellow onion, diced

2 celery stalks, diced

12 ounces mushrooms,
such as button or cremini,
thinly sliced

2 cloves garlic, minced

I cup white wine

2 cups chicken stock

I pound carrots, cut diagonally
into 2-inch pieces about
½-inch thick

5 sprigs thyme

I bay leaf

I tablespoon unsalted butter

I tablespoon sherry vinegar

Chopped fresh flat-leaf
parsley, for garnish

This version of coq au vin is familiar and comforting but has been brightened up a bit by a simple swap: white wine for red. Bacon adds a lovely smoky note, and the fat aids in browning the chicken and vegetables. If you don't want to use bacon, you can swap in 2 tablespoons olive oil. This recipe loves cast iron, since it starts and finishes on the stovetop with oven braising in between. Consider serving the coq au vin over Creamy Rosemary Polenta (page 35).

Preheat the oven to 350°F.

In a large cast-iron cocotte, cook the bacon over medium heat until browned and the fat is rendered, about 5 minutes. Remove the bacon to a paper towel–lined plate.

Sprinkle the chicken with salt and pepper. Working in batches, brown the chicken, skin-side down, for 3 to 5 minutes, or until the chicken skin is golden brown. Remove from the pan to a plate and set aside.

Carefully remove all but 2 tablespoons fat from the pan. Add the onion, celery, and mushrooms and cook until softened, 4 to 6 minutes. Add the garlic and cook for another 30 seconds, or until aromatic. Deglaze the pot with the wine. Add the stock, carrots, thyme, bay leaf, and a big pinch each of salt and pepper. Return the bacon to the pot and nestle the chicken into the braising liquid. Cover, transfer to the oven, and cook for 1½ hours, or until the chicken is fork-tender.

Remove the chicken from the cocotte to a baking sheet fitted with a wire rack. Place the cocotte on the stovetop over medium-high heat and reduce the sauce by half, about 5 minutes. Stir in the butter and sherry vinegar, taste, and add more salt if needed. Return the chicken and any accumulated juices to the cocotte and cook to warm through. Spoon into bowls and serve garnished with parsley.

CHICKEN MEATBALLS IN RED COCONUT CURRY SAUCE FROM EDWARD LEE OF 610 MAGNOLIA, MILKWOOD, SUCCOTASH, AND WHISKEY DRY

MAKES 4 SERVINGS

I pound ground chicken

3 ounces daikon radish, finely grated

5 cloves garlic, minced

4 teaspoons toasted sesame oil

2 teaspoons soy sauce

2 teaspoons whole milk

I teaspoon Worcestershire sauce

I teaspoon maple syrup

½ teaspoon fish sauce

¾ teaspoon salt

Freshly ground black pepper

3 green onions, finely chopped

About ¼ cup grapeseed oil

2 teaspoons grapeseed oil

2 shallots, minced

2 lemongrass stalks, finely chopped

2 tablespoons minced fresh ginger

2 small dried chiles de árbol

2 tablespoons soy sauce

I tablespoon fish sauce

I teaspoon ground cumin

I teaspoon ground coriander

½ teaspoon paprika

½ teaspoon grated nutmeg

½ teaspoon ground turmeric

I cup unsweetened coconut milk

Salt

Brooklyn-born and Louisville-made chef Edward Lee is famous for his inventive Southern and Asian mashups. Here he pushes the boundaries of ordinary chicken meatballs by serving them in a fragrant and tasty coconut curry sauce. Made with aromatic lemongrass, pungent fish sauce, sweet maple syrup, and salty Worcestershire, this original sauce makes this a delicious dish to serve on repeat. These are delicious served over rice with lime wedges and fresh cliantro.

Make the meatballs: In a medium bowl, combine the chicken, daikon, 1 clove garlic, sesame oil, soy sauce, milk, Worcestershire sauce, maple syrup, fish sauce, salt, pepper, and green onions. Using your hands, mix the ingredients together well and form the mixture into bite-size meatballs.

Heat a large cast-iron fry pan over medium heat. Add 1 tablespoon grapeseed oil to the pan, place about 6 meatballs into the pan, and pan-fry for 4 minutes, turning occasionally, or until meatballs are browned on all sides. Transfer to a paper towel–lined plate to drain. Repeat to cook the remaining meatballs, adding more oil to the pan with each batch.

Carefully wipe out the pan with a paper towel and make the sauce: Heat the grapeseed oil over medium heat. Add the shallots, remaining garlic, lemongrass, and ginger and cook, stirring, until softened, about 3 minutes. Add the chiles, soy sauce, fish sauce, cumin, coriander, paprika, nutmeg, and turmeric and cook until fragrant, about 3 minutes. Stir in the coconut milk. Transfer to a blender and blend until smooth. Return the sauce to the fry pan and bring to a simmer over medium heat. Add the meatballs and toss to coat them in the sauce. Simmer until the sauce thickens, 3 to 4 minutes. Season with salt. Transfer the meatballs and sauce to a platter and serve.

DUNGENESS CRAB STEW WITH FENNEL AND CITRUS FROM JONATHAN WAXMAN OF BARBUTO

MAKES 6 TO 8 SERVINGS

¼ cup olive oil

1 head garlic, cut in half horizontally

2 onions, sliced

2 leeks, white and light green parts, cut in half lengthwise and sliced

1 bulb fennel, cored and thinly sliced

2 bay leaves

Peel of 2 oranges

3 Roma tomatoes, diced

1 teaspoon grated fresh ginger

¼ teaspoon red pepper flakes

Pinch of saffron

2 cups rosé wine

1 pound halibut, skin removed and cut into 8 cubes

1 pound unpeeled whole head-on shrimp

Salt and freshly ground black pepper

¼ cup unsalted butter

2 cooked Dungeness crabs, cut in half and gills removed

This seafood stew is emblematic of chef Jonathan Waxman's ingredient-driven, Italian/Cali/French fare that lures diners to his restaurants in New York, Atlanta, Nashville, and counting. Waxman brightens a traditional garlicky-tomato broth with fennel, orange zest, and rosé—one aromatic spoonful will whisk you away to the Mediterranean. Seafood stew might sound fancy, but this one couldn't be easier to make. The recipe calls for cooked crab, as it is most readily available, but if you have access to fresh crab, by all means use it; add it with the wine to cook it through. Serve with rice, orzo, or crusty bread and, naturally, a bottle of dry rosé.

In a large cast-iron cocotte, heat the oil over medium-high heat. Add the garlic, onions, leeks, and fennel. Cook for 3 to 5 minutes, or until soft, then add the bay leaves, orange peel, tomatoes, ginger, red pepper flakes, saffron, and wine and bring to a simmer.

Add the halibut and shrimp and a large pinch each of salt and pepper and stir well with a wooden spoon. Cover and cook for 8 minutes, or until the fish and shrimp are just about cooked through. Add the butter and crabs, cover again, and cook until the crabs are warmed through. Serve immediately.

BRUNSWICK STEW

FROM AMANDA HESSER AND MERRILL STUBBS OF FOOD52

3 pounds boneless pork butt, cut into 4 smaller pieces

8 cups homemade or good-quality store-bought low-sodium chicken stock

3 ounces pancetta

3 medium carrots, cut into ½-inch rounds

1 large yellow onion, finely chopped

1 (28-ounce) can crushed tomatoes with their juices

¾ cup Carolina vinegar-based barbecue sauce

6 tablespoons Worcestershire sauce

Kosher salt

Freshly ground black pepper

1½ teaspoons ground cayenne

4 ears corn, kernels removed from the cob

12 ounces cooked lima beans (frozen is fine)

8 ounces fresh okra (optional)

2 tablespoons unsalted butter

This humble stew has inspired years of fierce debate: Brunswick, Virginia, and Brunswick, Georgia, both lay claim to it, and each state has its own defining characteristics. Legend tells of rabbit, possum, and even squirrel, but nowadays chicken is standard in both varieties, typically in a tomato base with lima beans or butter beans, corn, and okra.

In this recipe from Food52, the popular community cooking site, the stew hews more closely to the Georgian model, which often calls for pork as well as chicken and is chunkier than the Virginian version. But they decided to skip the poultry altogether, instead highlighting one of their favorite cuts of meat, pork butt. This is a meal in itself, but it won't suffer from a side of homemade Toasty Honey Corn Loaf (page 72).

In an extra large cast-iron cocotte, combine the pork, chicken stock, and pancetta and bring to a boil. Cover, reduce the heat, and simmer for 2 hours. Add the carrots, onion, crushed tomatoes, barbecue sauce, Worcestershire sauce, 2 teaspoons salt, ½ teaspoon black pepper, and the cayenne and stir to combine. Return to a simmer and continue to simmer for 1 hour more. Add the corn and lima beans and simmer for an additional hour, or until the pork is fork-tender.

Meanwhile, trim the stem ends of the okra and slice it into ½-inch pieces. Bring a medium cocotte of salted water to a rolling boil, add the okra, and cook for 8 to 10 minutes, until just tender. Drain and set aside.

Transfer the pork from the pot to a cutting board and shred it into large pieces. Return the meat to the stew, add the okra and the butter, and simmer for 15 more minutes. Taste and adjust the seasoning if necessary. Divide the stew among bowls and serve.

LAMB STEW WITH TURKISH BEANS AND PICKLED TOMATOES

FROM CHRISTOPHER KIMBALL OF CHRISTOPHER KIMBALL'S MILK STREET

MAKES 6 SERVINGS

PICKLED TOMATOES

3 plum tomatoes

3 tablespoons apple cider vinegar

1 tablespoon chopped dill

1 teaspoon Aleppo pepper

1 teaspoon sugar

½ teaspoon kosher salt

LAMB STEW

1 pound dried cannellini beans, soaked overnight in salted water and drained

1 (12- to 16-ounce) lamb shank

1 large yellow onion, chopped

¼ cup salted butter

8 cloves garlic, peeled and smashed

4 thyme sprigs

2 bay leaves

1 teaspoon paprika

1 teaspoon red pepper flakes

1 (14½-ounce) can diced tomatoes, drained

Kosher salt

½ cup chopped parsley

2 tablespoons chopped fresh dill, plus more for serving

2 tablespoons pomegranate molasses, plus more for serving

Freshly ground black pepper

FOR SERVING

Whole-milk yogurt

Olive oil

Longtime food personality Christopher Kimball has spent his career perfecting recipes to pass on to his fans. Lamb stew often conjures up ideas of heavy meals, but Kimball has a few genius ideas here for balancing the flavors. Pomegranate molasses adds a unique fruity sweetness, pickled tomatoes offer bright pops of flavor, and fresh dill lightens up lamb's richness. The creamy texture of dried cannellini beans is best for this recipe, but Great Northern beans can work in a pinch.

Make the pickled tomatoes: Core, seed, and dice the tomatoes. In a medium bowl, stir together the tomatoes, vinegar, dill, Aleppo pepper, sugar, and salt. Cover and refrigerate for at least 1 hour, until you are ready to serve.

Make the stew: Preheat the oven to 325°F.

In a large cast-iron cocotte, combine 5½ cups water, the beans, lamb shank, onion, butter, garlic, thyme, bay leaves, paprika, and red pepper flakes. Bring to a boil over high heat, then turn off the heat, cover, and transfer to the oven. Bake for 1 hour and 15 minutes. Stir in the tomatoes and 2 teaspoons salt. Return, uncovered, to the oven and bake until the beans are tender and creamy and the liquid is slightly thickened, about another 1 hour and 15 minutes. Transfer the cocotte to a wire rack. Remove the lamb shank to a bowl and set aside to cool. Discard the thyme sprigs and bay leaves. Let the beans sit for 20 minutes.

Remove the lamb meat from the bone, discarding the fat, gristle, and bone. Finely chop the meat and stir it into the beans. Stir in the parsley, dill, and molasses. Taste and season with salt and pepper as needed. Spoon into bowls and serve with yogurt, a drizzle of oil, some pomegranate molasses, dill, and the pickled tomatoes.

BEER-BRAISED SHORT RIBS

MAKES 6 TO 8 SERVINGS

2 tablespoons
dark brown sugar

I tablespoon smoked paprika

I tablespoon curry powder

2 teaspoons ground cumin

2 teaspoons salt

4 pounds bone-in short ribs,
cut into 4-inch pieces

3 tablespoons olive oil

I onion, diced

4 medium carrots, chopped

4 celery stalks, diced

4 cloves garlic, minced

I bay leaf

2 cups beef or chicken stock

I (12-ounce) bottle
brown ale or porter

I (28-ounce) can diced
tomatoes, with juices

This recipe is the ultimate cold-weather comfort, warming your body and your home with its rich flavors and aromas. The typical red wine is swapped for beer for a broader, earthier flavor. Seek out a brown ale or a porter, which provides richness without the bitterness associated with stout. Ask your butcher for bone-in short ribs that have been cut in half. Serve these short ribs over a big bowl of Creamy Rosemary Polenta (page 35) or with thick hunks of crusty bread to sop up the savory sauce.

Preheat the oven to 425°F.

In a small bowl, combine the brown sugar, smoked paprika, curry powder, cumin, and salt. Sprinkle the short ribs on all sides with the seasoning mixture. Lay on a baking sheet fitted with a wire rack and roast for 15 minutes. Remove from the oven and set aside.

Decrease the oven temperature to 350°F.

In an extra-large oval cast-iron cocotte, heat the oil over medium-high heat. Add the onion, carrots, and celery and cook for 5 to 7 minutes, until softened. Add the garlic and cook for another 30 seconds, or until aromatic. Add the bay leaf, stock, beer, and tomatoes and bring to a boil. Remove from the heat and nestle the short ribs into the braising liquid. Place in the oven, cover, and cook for 2 hours or until the meat is fork-tender, removing the lid for the last 30 minutes of cooking. Divide the short ribs among bowls and serve with a spoonful of the braising sauce.

BEEF BOURGUIGNON

MAKES 6 TO 8 SERVINGS

2½ pounds boneless beef chuck, cut into 1-inch cubes

¼ cup all-purpose flour

Salt and freshly ground black pepper

8 ounces bacon, diced

1 onion, diced

6 carrots, diced

4 celery stalks

1 pound cremini or button mushrooms, thinly sliced

2 cloves garlic, minced

½ cup cognac

2 cups dry red wine, such as Pinot Noir

2 cups beef stock

1 tablespoon tomato paste

1 teaspoon fresh thyme leaves, chopped

1 tablespoon brown sugar

Chopped fresh flat-leaf parsley, for garnish

This quintessential French dish is an essential to get through the winter. Beef simmers succulently in mushrooms, herbs, and red wine—*bourguignon* refers to Burgundy, France's famed wine region. Don't be intimidated by the number of ingredients—every step of this recipe happens in the same pan. That's why cast iron is choice, boasting both beautiful browning and braising capabilities, plus it holds in the heat of this comforting stew.

Preheat the oven to 350°F.

In a large bowl, toss the beef with the flour and a large pinch of salt and pepper. Set aside.

In a large cast-iron cocotte, render the fat from the bacon over medium-low heat until the edges of the bacon are crispy. Remove the bacon to a large bowl, leaving the rendered fat in the pan. Increase the heat to medium high. Add the beef to the fat in the pan and brown it on all sides. Remove the beef from the pan to the bowl with the bacon. Add the onion, carrots, celery, and mushrooms to the pan. Reduce the heat to medium and cook for 5 to 7 minutes, until softened. Add the garlic and cook for another 30 seconds, or until aromatic. Remove vegetables from the pan to the bowl with the beef.

Deglaze the pan with the cognac and cook until reduced by half, scraping the bottom of the pan to release any browned bits. Add the wine, stock, tomato paste, thyme, brown sugar, and a big pinch of salt and pepper. Bring to a boil, then remove from the heat. Return the bacon, beef, and vegetables to the pot, cover, and place in the oven. Cook for 1½ to 2 hours, until the beef is fork-tender. Remove from the oven, taste, and adjust the seasoning with salt and pepper if needed. Serve garnished with parsley.

MAIN COURSES

Sweet Potato Enchiladas with
Roasted Tomatillo Sauce 131

Kimchi Fried Rice 135

Chicken Pot Pie with
Phyllo Dough 136

Rosemary Buttermilk
Fried Chicken 139

Spatchcock Chicken with
Fresh Figs and Thyme 140

Braised Chicken Thighs with
Mushrooms and Madeira 142

One-Pan Chinese
Chicken and Rice 143

Roast Chicken with Fingerling
Potatoes, Herbs, and Lemon 144

Turkey Roulade with
Sage and Orange 147

Pan-Seared Salmon with Tomato
and Corn Salsa 148

Pan-Seared Scallops with Brown
Butter and Parsnip Puree 151

Salmon Burgers with
Sriracha Mayonnaise and
Pickled Cucumbers 152

New England Clam Bake 153

Thai Mussels with Coconut Milk
and Lemongrass 154

Olive Oil–Poached Tuna
with Blood Oranges and Fennel 157

Garlicky Pan-Seared Shrimp 158

Cider-Brined Pork Chops with
Apples and Balsamic Vinegar 161

Crispy Porchetta with Fennel
Seed and Citrus Zest 162

Bacon Chorizo Biryani 165

Choucroute Garnie 166

Confit Lamb with Rhubarb Mostarda
and Horseradish Gremolata 167

Black Pepper and Porcini–Crusted
Filet with Herbed Butter 168

Grilled Bone-In Rib Eye Topped with
Shallot Compote and Watercress 171

SWEET POTATO ENCHILADAS WITH ROASTED TOMATILLO SAUCE

2 pounds tomatillos, husks removed

I large onion or 2 small onions, quartered

4 cloves garlic, peeled

I green chile, such as Anaheim, quartered and seeded (optional)

¼ cup vegetable oil

Kosher salt and freshly ground black pepper

2 medium sweet potatoes (about I pound), peeled and diced

I teaspoon ground cumin

2 teaspoons chili powder

I cup chicken or vegetable stock

½ cup chopped fresh cilantro, plus more for garnish

I tablespoon fresh lime juice

8 ounces sharp cheddar cheese, grated

8 ounces mozzarella cheese, grated

I (15-ounce) can black beans, drained and rinsed

10 (6-inch) corn tortillas

FOR SERVING

Sour cream

Sweet potatoes are tossed with a roasted tomatillo sauce in these hearty and bright-tasting enchiladas. Tomatillos are generally available year-round in the produce section of your grocery store. Roasting the tomatillos, onion, garlic, and sweet potatoes simultaneously saves the time it takes to get dinner to the table. If you dice your sweet potatoes on the smaller side, dinner is ready even faster. Plus, the roasting adds the caramelized flavors that make these enchiladas so appealing.

Preheat the oven to 400°F.

On a baking sheet, combine the tomatillos, onion, garlic, and green chile. Toss with 2 tablespoons of the oil and a large pinch each of salt and pepper. On a separate baking sheet, toss the sweet potatoes with the remaining olive oil, cumin, chili powder, and a pinch each of salt and pepper. Roast the tomatillos and sweet potatoes for 30 to 35 minutes, tossing halfway through, until the vegetables are softened and lightly charred. Chop half of the roasted onion and 2 cloves of the roasted garlic, place them in a large bowl, and set aside.

Place the tomatillos and the remaining roasted vegetables in a blender along with a large pinch of salt, the stock, and cilantro. Blend until the tomatillos are broken down into a chunky sauce, then pour the sauce into a 12-inch cast-iron fry pan. Heat the sauce over medium heat until it is reduced slightly, 4 to 6 minutes. Turn off the heat and add the lime juice. Taste and add more salt if needed, then set aside.

In a medium bowl, combine the cheeses.

continued

Add the sweet potatoes and black beans to the bowl with the roasted onion and garlic. Fold in 1½ cups of the cheese mixture.

Remove all but ½ cup of the tomatillo sauce from the pan for serving and pour the remaining sauce into a shallow bowl.

Dip the tortillas into the sauce, fill each tortilla with about ½ cup of the filling, roll them up, and place them seam-side down into a large cast-iron fry pan. (Alternatively you can roll them and then spoon the sauce over the top.) Drizzle with the remaining ½ cup of the sauce and top with the remaining cheese. Cover and bake for 30 minutes, then uncover and bake for about 5 minutes more, until the cheese is melted and bubbly. Serve the enchiladas topped with sour cream and cilantro.

KIMCHI FRIED RICE

FROM ALANA KYSAR OF FIX FEAST FLAIR

2 tablespoons mild-flavored oil, such as grapeseed

1 onion, diced

1½ cups kimchi, roughly chopped

1 to 2 tablespoons gochujang

4 cups cooked day-old short-grain rice, at room temperature

2 tablespoons toasted sesame oil

½ cup chopped green onions

2 teaspoons soy sauce

Salt

FOR SERVING

Shredded nori seaweed

Toasted sesame seeds

Fried eggs (optional)

Alana Kysar, Hawaii native and founder of cooking lifestyle blog *Fix Feast Flair*, shares her family recipe for kimchi fried rice, a funky, fermented taste explosion. Kimchi, Korean-style fermented cabbage, can be found in many grocery stores and Asian markets in the refrigerator section. *Gochujang* is a Korean hot sauce; if unavailable, feel free to substitute your favorite hot sauce.

The key to perfect fried rice is using day-old rice so it can best absorb the flavors in the recipe. Top with a fried egg, or two, to make a meal out of it.

In a large cast-iron fry pan, heat the mild-flavored oil over medium heat. Add the onion and cook for 3 to 5 minutes, until translucent. Add the kimchi and gochujang and cook for 4 minutes, or until the liquid at the edges of the kimchi starts to simmer.

Meanwhile, toss the rice with the sesame oil. Add the rice and ¼ cup of the green onions to the the pan with the kimchi. Drizzle the soy sauce over the rice and stir-fry for 4 to 5 minutes, until the rice is hot and has absorbed all of the liquid. Taste and add salt if needed. Remove the pan from the heat, spoon into bowls or onto a plate, and top with the remaining ¼ cup green onions, some shredded nori, and sesame seeds. Top each bowl with a fried egg.

CHICKEN POT PIE WITH PHYLLO DOUGH

MAKES 4 TO 6 SERVINGS

I cup unsalted butter

½ cup all-purpose flour

¼ cup Madeira or dry vermouth

4 cups chicken stock

I large yellow onion, diced

4 celery stalks, thinly sliced

2 carrots, diced

1½ pounds small red-skinned potatoes, cut into ½-inch cubes

I bay leaf

1½ teaspoons curry powder

Salt and freshly ground black pepper

4 cups (I inch cubes) cooked chicken (about 1½ pounds)

I (I-pound) bag frozen peas

I (I-pound) box phyllo dough, defrosted

I large egg, whisked with 2 teaspoons water

When you want a big bowl of delicious heart-warming food, chicken pot pie is just the thing. This recipe looks really fancy, but it couldn't be simpler, as it uses store-bought phyllo dough, frozen peas, and already-cooked chicken. Phyllo dough topping gives a sophisticated twist to the classic, creating the perfect crust.

Preheat the oven to 350°F.

In a medium cast-iron cocotte, melt ½ cup of the butter over medium-low heat. Add the flour and whisk well. Add the Madeira and stock, stir well, and bring to a boil. Reduce the mixture slightly, until it coats the back of a spoon. Add the onion, celery, carrots, potatoes, bay leaf, and curry powder. Season with salt and pepper. Cover and cook until the vegetables are tender, 8 to 10 minutes. Remove the bay leaf and add the chicken and peas. Remove from the heat.

In a small fry pan, melt the remaining ½ cup butter over medium-low heat. Remove from the heat.

Spread the phyllo dough onto a clean surface and cut it in half crosswise. Return half of the phyllo to the freezer and save for another use. Place one piece of the remaining phyllo on the countertop. Using a pastry brush, brush the melted butter over the phyllo. Top with another piece of phyllo, placing it slightly off-center to create the start of a star shape. This will make it easier to place on top of the cocotte. Repeat with remaining sheets of phyllo.

Carefully pick up the phyllo and transfer it to the cocotte. Press the phyllo into the cocotte, keeping an overhang of phyllo on the sides of the pot. Brush the phyllo with the egg wash and carefully slice a slit in the top of the phyllo. Bake the chicken pot pie for 25 to 35 minutes, until the phyllo is golden brown. Let chicken pot pie rest for 10 minutes; serve warm.

ROSEMARY BUTTERMILK FRIED CHICKEN

4 cups buttermilk

1 tablespoon smoked paprika

1 tablespoon freshly ground black pepper

2 tablespoons salt

1 tablespoon honey

2 cloves garlic, smashed

2 sprigs rosemary

1 whole chicken (about 3½ pounds), cut into 10 pieces

3¼ cups all-purpose flour

¾ cup cornstarch

1½ teaspoons baking soda

Vegetable oil, for frying

Flaky sea salt

This recipe makes the most of an American classic. The chicken is marinated overnight in buttermilk, herbs, and spices for extra juiciness. Frying the chicken until crispy and then finishing it in the oven will prevent the coating from burning and will ensure the chicken is cooked through. This chicken goes great with Toasty Honey Corn Loaf (page 72) either hot or at room temperature. Why not pack them both up for a Southern-style picnic?

In a large bowl, whisk together the buttermilk, 1½ teaspoons of the smoked paprika, 1½ teaspoons of the black pepper, and 1 tablespoon of the salt. Whisk in the honey and garlic and add the rosemary. Add the chicken, cover, and marinate overnight or up to 24 hours.

When it's time to fry the chicken, make the coating. In a large bowl, combine the flour, cornstarch, the remaining 1½ teaspoons smoked paprika, the remaining 1½ teaspoons black pepper, the remaining 1 tablespoon salt, and the baking soda. Coat the chicken well and set the chicken on a baking sheet while the oil and oven preheat.

Preheat the oven to 350°F.

Fill a large cast-iron cocotte halfway with oil. Heat the oil over medium-high heat until it reaches 350°F on a deep-fry thermometer. Working in batches, carefully add the chicken to the cocotte, making sure not to overcrowd the pan. Fry the chicken for 6 to 8 minutes, until golden brown. As each batch is done, remove the chicken from the oil and place on a baking sheet fitted with a wire rack.

Once all the chicken is fried, put the chicken in the oven and bake for 10 to 12 minutes, until the internal temperature registers 165°F on a thermometer. Serve the chicken hot, warm, or at room temperature sprinkled with flaky sea salt.

SPATCHCOCK CHICKEN WITH FRESH FIGS AND THYME

MAKES 4 SERVINGS

1 (3½- to 4-pound) chicken, backbone removed

Salt and freshly ground black pepper

3 shallots, minced

2 cloves garlic

3 tablespoons sherry vinegar

½ cup chicken stock

8 ounces fresh figs, cut in half

1 tablespoon unsalted butter (optional)

1 teaspoon fresh thyme leaves, chopped

The term *spatchcock* might sound complicated, but basically it means a bird that has had its backbone removed and is flattened into one layer. This method allows for faster, more even cooking. And by increasing the surface area, you increase the amount of browned bits that make roast chicken so scrumptious. You can ask your butcher counter to remove the backbone for you. A pan sauce made with sherry vinegar and fresh figs creates a rich but balanced sauce to drizzle on the chicken. Don't forget to salt your chicken really well, as salt brings out the best in chicken.

Preheat the oven to 425°F. Place a large cast-iron fry pan in the oven while it is preheating.

Lay the chicken breast-side up on a cutting board. Using your hands, carefully press the chicken down into the cutting board, flattening it. Liberally sprinkle the chicken with salt and pepper.

Place the chicken, breast-side up, in the preheated fry pan. Place it in the oven and roast the chicken for about 45 minutes. Tent it with aluminum foil if the skin starts to get too dark. Cook until a meat thermometer reads 165°F when inserted into the deepest part of a thigh. Carefully remove the chicken from the pan and let it rest on a platter.

Carefully place the hot fry pan on the stovetop over low heat and add the shallots, garlic, vinegar, stock, and figs. Cook until the figs are warmed through and the liquid is reduced by one-third. Melt in the butter, add the thyme, and season with salt and pepper. Serve the chicken with the pan sauce.

BRAISED CHICKEN THIGHS WITH MUSHROOMS AND MADEIRA

MAKES 6 SERVINGS

6 bone-in, skin-on chicken thighs (about 2½ pounds)

Salt and freshly ground black pepper

2 tablespoons olive oil

I onion, diced

¾ cup sliced mushrooms, such as cremini or button mushrooms

2 cloves garlic, minced

¼ cup Madeira

I cup chicken stock

I tablespoon chopped fresh tarragon, plus more for garnish

Squeeze of lemon or splash of sherry vinegar

Braising is a home chef's secret weapon, an uncomplicated technique that creates complex, restaurant-quality flavors. Meat is first seared, then succulently simmered in wine, broth, or a mix of the two. Cast iron is the best tool for braising, with its browning and even-heating capabilities. In this recipe, chicken, mushrooms, and tarragon are a match made in heaven. Add Madeira, a fortified wine, to create a flavor-packed sauce. If you can't find Madeira, you can substitute marsala or white wine. Make sure the braising liquid doesn't cover the chicken skin on the thighs so the skin can get all sorts of crispy while it braises. Serve with Creamy Rosemary Polenta (page 35) and Artichokes à la Barigoule (page 45) for a sophisticated supper.

Preheat the oven to 350°F.

Sprinkle the chicken thighs with salt and pepper.

Heat the olive oil in a large cast-iron fry pan or braiser over medium-high heat. Add the chicken thighs, in batches if needed to prevent overcrowding, and cook until browned on both sides, 5 to 7 minutes. Remove from the pan and set aside on a plate.

Carefully pour all but 2 tablespoons fat from the pan. Add the onion and cook for 3 to 5 minutes, until it is soft and translucent. Add the mushrooms and cook for another 5 minutes, or until softened. Add the garlic and cook for 30 seconds, or until aromatic. Deglaze the pan with the Madeira and chicken stock and fold in the tarragon.

Return the chicken thighs to the pan, skin-side up. Roast in the oven for 25 to 30 minutes, until the internal temperature reads 165°F on an instant-read thermometer. Let rest for 5 minutes, then taste the sauce for salt and pepper and serve, garnished with tarragon and a squeeze of lemon.

ONE-PAN CHINESE CHICKEN AND RICE

FROM STEPHANIE LE OF I AM A FOOD BLOG

2 tablespoons grapeseed oil

6 bone-in, skin-on chicken thighs

4 links Chinese sausage, thinly sliced

2 cloves garlic, minced

I (½-inch) piece ginger, grated

I½ cups long-grain rice, such as jasmine

2 cups chicken stock

I tablespoon sweet soy sauce, plus more if needed

I tablespoon light soy sauce

I tablespoon dark soy sauce

I tablespoon oyster sauce

I tablespoon Shaoxing wine

I teaspoon sugar

I teaspoon toasted sesame oil

8 ounces fresh shiitake mushrooms, stemmed and thinly sliced

2 cups chopped baby bok choy, washed and trimmed

FOR SERVING

Hot sauce (optional)

This one-pan chicken and rice dish comes from Stephanie Le, a fun Chinese-Canadian writer who runs the gorgeous *I Am a Food Blog* with her husband, Mike. Her toothsome take on the classic chicken dinner includes three types of soy sauce: dark for molasses-like richness, sweet for maple-syrup-style sweetness, and light for delicate seasoning. Head to your local Asian market to find the soy sauce, the Chinese sausage, and the Shaoxing wine. If you don't have one nearby, you can definitely find the ingredients online. These elements add depth of flavor to the dish and are worth the extra effort to seek out. Plus, once you have them in your pantry, it will be even easier to make other Asian dishes.

In a cast-iron braiser or cocotte, heat the oil over medium-high heat until shimmering. Add the chicken thighs, skin-side down, and cook until deeply browned, 5 to 8 minutes. Stir in the sausage, flip the chicken pieces, and cook for another minute or two until the other side is browned. Remove the chicken and sausage from the pan to a plate, leaving the rendered fat in the pan.

Reduce the heat to medium, add the garlic and ginger, and cook, stirring, until softened, 1 to 2 minutes. Add the rice and stir until glossy and coated in the fat. Add the chicken stock, soy sauces, oyster sauce, wine, sugar, and toasted sesame oil, stirring to combine. Increase the heat to medium-high and bring to a boil. Add the mushrooms, chicken, and sausage to the pan. Reduce the heat to low, cover, and cook for 15 to 20 minutes, or until the rice is cooked through and the chicken registers 165°F on a meat thermometer. Add the bok choy, cover again, and cook for 5 minutes, or until the bok choy is softened. Remove from the heat and let rest for 10 minutes, keeping the lid on. Serve with hot sauce and extra sweet soy sauce, if needed.

ROAST CHICKEN WITH FINGERLING POTATOES, HERBS, AND LEMON

MAKES 4 TO 6 SERVINGS

1 (3½- to 4-pound) chicken

Salt

1½ pounds fingerling potatoes, cut in half lengthwise if large

3 tablespoons olive oil

Freshly ground black pepper

1 lemon, cut in half

1 head of garlic, cut in half, horizontally

1 red onion, peeled and quartered

1 tablespoon assorted chopped fresh herbs, such as thyme and rosemary

¼ cup unsalted butter, at room temperature

It's pretty hard to beat a perfectly roasted chicken. This recipe is inspired by the famous roast chicken at the San Francisco restaurant Zuni Café, where their secret is to salt the raw chicken up to seventy-two hours before roasting. This method, called salt brining, creates a deliciously moist chicken because the salt draws out moisture that dissolves the crystals, then the bird reabsorbs this salty liquid down to the bone. This recipe calls for salting for just twenty-four hours, and if you don't have that much time, as little as thirty minutes will have an effect.

Place the chicken on a baking sheet fitted with a wire rack. Liberally sprinkle salt all over the chicken, loosely cover the chicken with parchment paper, and refrigerate for 24 hours.

Preheat the oven to 500°F. Let the chicken come to room temperature for about 30 minutes before roasting.

In a medium bowl, toss the potatoes with 2 tablespoons of the oil and a big pinch of salt and pepper. Arrange the potatoes in a single layer in the bottom of a large cast-iron cocotte. Add the lemon halves, garlic halves, and red onion quarters. Drizzle with the remaining 1 tablespoon oil.

In a small bowl, stir the herbs into the butter. Gently separate the chicken skin from the meat and rub the butter mixture under and on top of the skin and all over the thighs and breasts. Place the chicken on top of the vegetables in the cocotte and roast for 20 minutes. Decrease the oven temperature to 350°F and continue roasting for 30 to 40 minutes, until a meat thermometer reads 165°F when inserted between the thigh and the breast.

Remove the chicken from the oven, tent with aluminum foil, and allow the chicken to rest for at 10 minutes before carving and serving.

TURKEY ROULADE WITH SAGE AND ORANGE

MARINADE

2 tablespoons chopped fresh sage

2 tablespoons orange zest

1 tablespoon honey

1 tablespoon kosher salt

1 teaspoon freshly ground black pepper

2 shallots, minced

2 cloves garlic, minced

¼ cup olive oil

1 whole turkey breast (about 5 pounds), boned and butterflied

FILLING

2 tablespoons olive oil

2 onions, diced

3 carrots, diced

3 celery stalks, diced

Kosher salt and freshly ground pepper

2 garlic cloves

¼ cup white wine

In this recipe, the turkey is marinated overnight in aromatic orange zest, garlic, and sage, rolled up to hold in the flavor while it cooks, then sliced and placed on a platter. This effortlessly elegant recipe can be served year-round, not just for the holidays.

To make the marinade: In a medium bowl, combine the sage, orange zest, honey, salt, pepper, shallots, garlic, and olive oil. Mix well and set aside.

Place turkey breast in a large container. Pour the marinade over the turkey breast and rub the marinade completely over the turkey breast. Cover with plastic wrap and refrigerate overnight. Remove the turkey breast and allow it to come to room temperature for 30 minutes.

In a large cast-iron skillet, make the filling by warming the olive oil over medium heat. Add the onions, carrots, celery, and a big pinch of salt and pepper. Cook over medium low until carrots are soft and the onions are translucent, about 20 to 25 minutes. Add in minced garlic and cook for another 30 seconds. Deglaze the pan with white wine and continue cooking until the wine has evaporated. Remove from heat and set aside.

Preheat oven to 350°F.

Lay the turkey breast-side down on a cutting board. Spread the filling in an even layer, leaving a ½-inch border on all sides. Roll the turkey breast up lengthwise. Flip the turkey breast over and tie with butcher's twine.

Place in a 10 by 15-inch rectangular roasting pan and cook for 1½ to 2 hours or until a meat thermometer reads 165°F. Begin checking on the turkey about 1 hour into the roasting time.

Remove the turkey breast from the pan and cover with tin foil and let rest for at least 15 minutes before slicing and serving. Sprinkle with flaky sea salt and serve warm.

PAN-SEARED SALMON
WITH TOMATO AND CORN SALSA

MAKES 4 SERVINGS

I cup cherry tomatoes,
cut in half

I cup fresh corn kernels
(from about 2 ears)

I avocado, pitted and diced

¼ cup red onion, minced

½ cup chopped fresh basil

Juice of I lime

3 tablespoons olive oil

Salt and freshly ground
black pepper

4 (6-ounce) skin-on salmon
fillets, pin bones removed

Here are two tips for perfectly cooked fish with the crispiest skin
ever. First, press out any excess moisture so the skin will crisp and not
steam. Second, get your cast-iron pan really hot and be liberal with oil.
In this recipe, salmon is topped with a best-of-the-summer salsa made
from tomatoes, corn, and basil. Make the salsa without the avocado
ahead of time, then when ready to serve, cook the fish and fold in the
avocado.

In a medium bowl, combine the cherry tomatoes, corn, avocado, red
onion, basil, lime juice, 1 tablespoon of the oil, and pinch of salt and
pepper. Toss well and set aside.

Heat a medium cast-iron fry pan over medium-high heat and add the
remaining 2 tablespoons oil.

Pat the salmon skin dry with a paper towel. Gently run a knife along the
skin, removing excess moisture but being careful not to cut the skin.
Season with salt and pepper.

Place 2 of the fillets in the pan, skin-side down, and cook for 3 to 4 minutes,
then flip and cook for 1 minute more, or until a paring knife can be easily
inserted without any resistance. Remove the salmon from the pan and let it
rest, covered with foil, while you cook the remaining 2 fillets. Arrange the
salmon on plates, top with the salsa, and serve immediately.

PAN-SEARED SCALLOPS WITH BROWN BUTTER AND PARSNIP PUREE

MAKES 4 TO 6 SERVINGS

½ cup unsalted butter

I pound parsnips, peeled and cut into I-inch pieces

I cup heavy cream

2 cloves garlic

2 sprigs thyme

I bay leaf

Kosher salt and freshly ground black pepper

2 tablespoons grapeseed oil

I pound scallops

Flaky sea salt

Scallops cook really quickly and are easier to prepare than shrimp (no shelling or deveining is required). The best way to prepare scallops is to sear them in a really hot pan for only a couple minutes on each side to give them a golden-brown crust without overcooking them. When bathed in a brown butter sauce and served atop a creamy parsnip puree, all these scallops need are sautéed greens and a glass of Chenin Blanc for a light, lovely meal. It's also helpful to add the scallops to the fry pan in a circular fashion, so that you can easily flip them over in the same order for even cooking.

In a small cast-iron fry pan, melt the butter over low heat, then continue to cook for 4 to 6 minutes, until the butter separates and the milk fats turn golden brown. Remove from the heat and set aside.

Put the parsnips in a medium cast-iron cocotte and add water to cover. Bring to a boil over medium-high heat and cook until the parsnips are very tender, 10 to 12 minutes. Drain.

While the parsnips are cooking, combine the cream, garlic, thyme, and bay leaf in a petite French oven and bring to a simmer over medium heat. Keep warm.

Place the parsnips in a blender or food processor. Strain the cream mixture, add half of it to the parsnips, and blend until smooth and creamy, adding more of the cream mixture as needed. Add a large pinch of salt and pepper, taste, and add more salt if needed. Keep warm.

Heat a medium cast-iron fry pan over medium-high heat until very hot. Add the oil, then add the scallops and sear for 1 to 2 minutes on each side, until golden brown. Serve the scallops with a dollop of the parsnip puree, a drizzle of brown butter, and a sprinkle of flaky sea salt.

SALMON BURGERS WITH SRIRACHA MAYONNAISE AND PICKLED CUCUMBERS

MAKES 4 SERVINGS

½ cup mayonnaise

I tablespoon sriracha

1½ pounds skinless salmon fillets, cut into I-inch pieces

¼ cup fresh cilantro leaves, plus more for garnish

2 tablespoons hoisin sauce

6 green onions, white and light green parts, thinly sliced

2 teaspoons grated peeled fresh ginger

⅓ cup panko bread crumbs

Salt

½ teaspoon freshly ground black pepper

½ English cucumber, thinly sliced

2 tablespoons rice vinegar

3 tablespoons toasted sesame oil

4 hamburger buns

Salmon burgers are the lighter but just as delicious cousin to the hamburger. These are filled with Asian flavors, like ginger and hoisin, and are tastily topped with spicy mayonnaise and pickled cucumbers for creaminess and crunch. Note that the salmon mixture will be very sticky as you form the patties, but it will all come together on the cast-iron grill pan. To make your salmon burgers gluten-free, swap gluten-free bread crumbs for the panko and serve on gluten-free buns.

In a small bowl, combine the mayonnaise and sriracha to taste. Set aside.

In the bowl of a food processor, combine the salmon, cilantro, hoisin sauce, green onions, ginger, panko, 1 teaspoon salt, the pepper, and 2 tablespoons of the sriracha mayonnaise and pulse until the ingredients are combined but the salmon is still slightly chunky. Form the salmon mixture into four ½-inch-thick patties. Place on a plate, cover with plastic wrap, and refrigerate for at least 2 hours or overnight.

While the salmon patties are chilling, make the pickled cucumbers: In a medium bowl, combine the cucumber, vinegar, and sesame oil. Season with salt and set aside.

Heat a cast-iron grill pan over medium-high heat until barely smoking. Add the patties and grill until the fish is cooked through, about 3 minutes per side. Toast the hamburger buns while the burgers rest.

To serve, spread the sriracha mayonnaise on one side of the hamburger buns and top with a salmon patty, cucumber salad, and cilantro leaves. Add the top bun and serve.

NEW ENGLAND CLAM BAKE

FROM MARCUS WARE OF GREYDON HOUSE

MAKES 4 SERVINGS

1½ pounds fingerling potatoes, scrubbed

2 tablespoons unsalted butter

Sea salt

1 tablespoon olive oil

1 onion, thinly sliced

1 head garlic, cloves peeled

1 sprig thyme

1 bay leaf

1 stalk lemongrass, white and light green parts, minced

1 cup white wine

2 cups fish stock

1 cup heavy cream

1 (1¼-pound) lobster

2 king crab legs

1 pound clams, scrubbed

1 pound mussels, cleaned and debearded

2 ears of corn, cut into thirds

1 bunch carrots, cut diagonally into 1-inch pieces

12 ounces andouille sausage, grilled, then diagonally sliced

4 ounces seaweed, such as kombu, soaked and chopped (optional)

3 tablespoons chopped fresh flat-leaf parsley

FOR SERVING

Grilled bread

This clambake comes from one of New England's loveliest spots, Nantucket. In this recipe, chef Marcus Ware, of the Greydon House hotel and restaurant, includes everything you love about summer at the beach, plus the untraditional addition of lemongrass to make the dish stand out. Serve family-style in the middle of the table, or break it down into individual portions.

Preheat the oven to 400°F.

Cut the ends off the potatoes to make a flat surface on both ends. Add the butter and a large pinch of salt to a small oval cast-iron roasting pan and arrange the potatoes in it so they are standing. Cover and cook over medium heat for 10 to 15 minutes, until golden brown. Flip the potatoes and cook for another 10 to 15 minutes, until the second side is golden brown and the potatoes are cooked through. Keep warm until ready to serve.

Heat the oil in a large cast-iron cocotte over a medium-low heat. Add the onion and a pinch of salt and cook until softened, about 10 minutes. Add the garlic, thyme, bay leaf, and lemongrass and cook for an additional 2 minutes. Add the wine, bring to a boil, then add the fish stock and cream and bring back to a boil. Decrease the heat to maintain a simmer. Season with salt.

Add the lobster and crab legs to the center of the pot. Next, add the clams, mussels, corn, carrots, and grilled sausage. Cover with the seaweed, place the lid on top, and place in the oven. Bake for 20 to 25 minutes, until the mussels and clams have opened and the lobster is bright pink. Discard any mussels and clams that didn't open. Remove from the oven and sprinkle with the parsley. Serve with the potatoes and grilled bread.

THAI MUSSELS WITH COCONUT MILK AND LEMONGRASS

MAKES 4 SERVINGS

1 tablespoon canola or vegetable oil

2 cloves garlic, minced

2 teaspoons grated peeled fresh ginger

1 large shallot, minced

1 (4-inch) piece lemongrass, white and light green parts, thinly sliced

1 Thai chile (optional)

1 tablespoon green curry paste

1 (15-ounce) can coconut milk

1 tablespoon fish sauce, plus more to taste

1½ to 2 pounds mussels, scrubbed and beards removed

Juice of 1 lime

Chopped fresh cilantro, for garnish

There are a few rules for cooking with mussels. First, throw away any mussels that are already opened when you purchase them. Second, use a paring knife to remove the fibrous strings on the outside of the mussels—called the "beard"—as they are tough. Third, discard any mussels that haven't opened during cooking. Last, always serve mussels with a crusty bread, coconut rice, or another starch to mop up all the delicious sauce. Mussels cook up quickly, making them ideal for a weeknight meal or a dinner party when you want to spend time with your guests instead of in the kitchen.

In a small cast-iron cocotte or mussel pot, combine the oil, garlic, ginger, shallot, lemongrass, and chile. Place over medium heat and cook for 1 to 2 minutes, until the shallot is translucent. Add the curry paste and cook for 30 seconds. Add the coconut milk and fish sauce, stir to combine, then add the mussels. Cover and cook for about 5 minutes, shaking the pan as the mussels cook, until they have opened.

Discard any mussels that do not open. Taste and add more fish sauce if needed. Serve family-style or spoon into bowls with a squeeze of lime juice and a sprinkle of cilantro.

OLIVE OIL–POACHED TUNA WITH BLOOD ORANGES AND FENNEL

4 cups olive oil

3 sprigs fresh herbs, such as rosemary or thyme

3 cloves unpeeled garlic

Red pepper flakes

4 (6-ounce) ahi tuna steaks (about 1 inch thick)

3 blood oranges, peeled

2 bulbs fennel, cut in half lengthwise, cored, and thinly sliced

¼ cup roughly chopped fresh flat-leaf parsley

2 tablespoons white wine vinegar

Salt and freshly ground black pepper

Flaky sea salt

Poaching tuna in olive oil creates a perfect steak that's cooked on the outside and pink and tender on the inside. Seek out a trusted fishmonger to source your tuna, as tuna is often overfished and color can be added to give the flesh a more vibrant pink color. When you poach the steaks, make sure they are covered in oil, and keep an eye on the temperature of your oil. Cast iron retains heat really well, so the temperature of the oil can get too high if left unmonitored. In this recipe, the tuna is topped with a winning Sicilian combo of raw fennel and blood oranges. If blood oranges are not in season, swap in Cara Cara or another type of orange.

In a medium cast-iron cocotte, combine the oil, herbs, garlic, and a pinch of red pepper flakes. Heat over medium-low heat until the oil reaches 200°F to 215°F on a deep-fry thermometer.

Slice the blood oranges over a small bowl, catching the juices in the bowl. Add the fennel, parsley, vinegar, and 2 to 3 tablespoons of the poaching liquid. Season with salt and pepper.

Gently lower 2 tuna steaks into the oil and cook for 4 to 6 minutes, until the tuna is lightly browned on the outside and still pink on the inside. Using a slotted spoon or spatula, remove the steaks to a plate and repeat with the remaining steaks.

Slice the tuna and serve the salad over the tuna. Serve hot or at room temperature, sprinkled with flaky salt.

GARLICKY PAN-SEARED SHRIMP

FROM JULIA TURSHEN, AUTHOR OF *SMALL VICTORIES*, *FEED THE RESISTANCE*, AND *NOW & AGAIN*

MAKES 4 TO 6 SERVINGS

2 pounds medium shrimp, peeled and deveined

3 tablespoons olive oil

I teaspoon salt

2 tablespoons unsalted butter

5 cloves garlic, minced

½ teaspoon red pepper flakes

3 tablespoons fresh lemon juice

Handful of chopped fresh flat-leaf parsley

Best-selling cookbook author Julia Turshen brings us this simple scampi-style recipe. She uses a searing-hot pan to quickly cook the shrimp, then tosses the shrimp with butter, garlic, lemon juice, and parsley. This dish is perfect for a summertime barbecue but if you don't have an outdoor grill, you can easily make it in a 450°F oven. Just preheat the fry pan in the hot oven, and complete the recipe in the oven. Serve with a starch, like spaghetti or sourdough bread, to soak up the finger-licking good sauce.

In a large bowl, combine the shrimp, oil, and salt and use your hands to coat the shrimp evenly.

Place a large cast-iron fry pan on an outdoor grill set to high heat (if using gas, or build a hot bed of coals if using charcoal) and heat until smoking hot. Add the shrimp to the pan in a single layer. Cook the shrimp without disturbing them until the undersides are dark golden brown and crispy, about 3 minutes.

Carefully flip each shrimp over and add the butter, garlic, and red pepper flakes to the pan. Once the butter melts and the garlic begins to sizzle, in about 30 seconds, take the pan off the heat. Stir well to coat the shrimp with the garlicky butter. Add the lemon juice and parsley to the pan and stir well to combine. Serve immediately.

CIDER-BRINED PORK CHOPS WITH APPLES AND BALSAMIC VINEGAR

BRINE

4 cups apple cider

2 tablespoons kosher salt

1 tablespoon whole peppercorns

1 bay leaf

2 teaspoons whole cloves

4 (8-ounce) bone-in center-cut pork chops (about 1 inch thick)

APPLE TOPPING

2 tablespoons olive oil

1 shallot, minced

3 firm, tart apples, such as Granny Smith or Honeycrisp, cored and cut into thin slices

¼ cup white balsamic vinegar

¼ cup apple cider

1 tablespoon brown sugar

Pinch of freshly grated nutmeg

Kosher salt and freshly ground black pepper

1 tablespoon whole-grain mustard

Olive oil, for cooking

Flaky sea salt

There are two crucial steps to making flavorful, juicy pork chops. First, always use bone-in pork chops, as the bone helps the meat retain moisture while boosting its flavor. The second step is to brine the pork chops to amp up the juiciness and add seasoning.

Brine the pork chops: In a medium cast-iron cocotte, combine 1 cup of the cider, the kosher salt, peppercorns, bay leaf, and cloves. Bring to a boil over medium heat, stirring to dissolve the kosher salt. Add the remaining 3 cups cider, cool to room temperature, then transfer to a large bowl or heavy-duty zip-top bag. Add the pork chops, cover, and refrigerate overnight.

Make the apple topping: In a medium cast-iron cocotte, heat the oil over medium heat. Add the shallot and cook until translucent, about 1 minute. Add the apples and cook for 1 to 2 minutes or until apples have begun to caramelize. Deglaze the pan with the vinegar and apple cider. Add the brown sugar and nutmeg and season with kosher salt and pepper. Bring to a boil, then reduce the heat to low and cook until the apples are softened but not falling apart. Stir in the mustard and keep warm.

Remove the pork chops from the brine and pat them dry with paper towels. In a large cast-iron fry pan, heat 2 tablespoons oil over medium-high heat. Add 2 pork chops and cook for about 6 minutes, flipping halfway through, until a meat thermometer reads 145°F. Repeat with the remaining pork chops, adding more oil to the pan as needed.

Remove the pork chops to a plate as they are done, tent them with foil, and allow them to rest for 5 minutes. Serve the pork chops with a scoop of the apple topping and a sprinkle of flaky sea salt.

CRISPY PORCHETTA WITH FENNEL SEED AND CITRUS ZEST

2 tablespoons fennel seeds

2 teaspoons coriander seeds

½ teaspoon red pepper flakes

1 teaspoon freshly ground black pepper

1 tablespoon lemon zest

2 tablespoons orange zest

2 tablespoons orange juice

2 cloves garlic, minced

1 tablespoon minced fresh sage

1 tablespoon minced fresh rosemary

Kosher salt

1 (5-pound) skin-on pork belly

1 (2- to 3-pound) pork tenderloin

Porchetta might sound exotic, but it is really easy to make. The biggest challenge is finding a butcher that carries pork belly. If you plan in advance, you can ask the butcher counter at your grocery store to order some, or seek out a specialty butcher that has a variety of cuts in stock. When roasted at high heat, the porchetta is cracklingly crispy on the outside and mouthwateringly tender on the inside.

In a small cast-iron fry pan, combine the fennel seeds, coriander seeds, and red pepper flakes. Toast over low heat for 1 to 2 minutes, until fragrant. Using a mortar and pestle or a spice grinder, grind the spices to a powder.

In a small bowl, combine the ground spices, the black pepper, lemon zest, orange zest, orange juice, garlic, sage, rosemary, and a large pinch of kosher salt. Set aside.

Lay the pork belly, skin-side up, on a cutting board. Using a paring knife, score the skin in a checkerboard pattern. Liberally sprinkle with kosher salt. Flip the pork belly over and poke holes into the meat using a wooden skewer, being careful not to poke all the way through the skin. Using a meat mallet or rolling pin, tenderize the meat for 2 to 3 minutes.

Sprinkle half of the herb mixture over the pork belly, then lay the tenderloin on the meat and spread the remaining herbs over it. Roll the pork belly around the tenderloin and tie with butcher's twine. Refrigerate uncovered overnight, occasionally blotting the skin dry with paper towels.

The next day, preheat the oven to 450°F.

Place the pork in a large cast-iron cocotte or roasting pan and roast for 45 minutes. Decrease the oven temperature to 325°F and continue roasting for 1 to 1½ hours, until a meat thermometer reads 145°F. Let the porchetta rest for 30 minutes before slicing and serving.

BACON CHORIZO BIRYANI

FROM FLOYD CARDOZ OF BOMBAY BREAD BAR

MAKES 6 TO 8 SERVINGS

8 ounces fingerling potatoes

2 tablespoons olive oil

½ cup cipollini onions

8 ounces bacon lardons
(¼ inch thick and 1 inch long)

½ cinnamon stick

3 whole cloves

1 onion, diced

1 bay leaf

2 cups diced tomatoes

12 ounces cooked chorizo,
diced

3 cups chicken stock

1½ cups basmati rice, rinsed

2 green onions, white and
light green parts, thinly sliced

Chef Floyd Cardoz serves Indian heritage through a modern American lens at his popular New York City spot, Bombay Bread Bar. Biryani is a one-pot South Asian rice dish typically made with warming spices and a protein such as chicken. Cardoz's vibrantly flavored biryani is spiced with cinnamon, cloves, and bay leaf and uses bacon and chorizo as proteins. Chorizo, or chouriço, is actually prominent in India's former Portuguese colony, Goa. Use cured and ready-to-eat chorizo, and if you can't find fresh cipollini onions, check the frozen vegetable section of your grocery store.

Preheat the oven to 350°F.

On a baking sheet, toss the potatoes with oil and roast for about 10 minutes. Add the cipollini onions and continue roasting until the potatoes are cooked through and firm but tender, about 10 minutes. Remove from the oven (leaving the oven on) and set aside to cool slightly, then remove the skins from the onions and slice the potatoes and onions in half lengthwise. Set aside.

Place a large cast-iron cocotte over medium heat and add the bacon. Cook until the bacon is crispy and the fat is rendered, about 8 minutes. Add the cinnamon stick and cloves and cook for about 1 minute, until fragrant. Add the onion and cook, stirring often, until softened, 4 to 6 minutes. Add the bay leaf, tomatoes, chorizo, cippolini onions, and potatoes to the pot, then add the chicken stock and bring to a boil. Fold in the rice, cover, and place in the oven. Bake for 30 minutes, or until the rice is cooked through and the water is absorbed. Sprinkle with the green onions and serve immediately.

CHOUCROUTE GARNIE

FROM SEAN PHARR OF MINT MARK

4 ounces bacon, diced

3 pounds boneless pork shoulder

2 onions, thinly sliced

4 cloves garlic, minced

4 pounds sauerkraut

1 teaspoon ground juniper berries

1 teaspoon ground caraway

3 bay leaves

1 teaspoon freshly ground black pepper

Salt

1 cup dry white wine, such as Riesling

3 cups chicken stock

3 pounds red potatoes, peeled

6 bratwurst sausages

FOR SERVING

Assorted mustards, such as Dijon, whole-grain, brown, and tarragon

Warm marbled rye bread

This traditional French food originated in the same region where Staub was born: Alsace. Francis Staub's benchmark cocotte was inspired by the one-pot dishes so prevalent throughout the German-influenced area. One of them, choucroute garnie, is shared here in a recipe by Sean Pharr, the executive chef and owner of Mint Mark in Madison, Wisconsin.

Preheat the oven to 300°F.

Heat a medium cast-iron cocotte over medium-high heat. Add the bacon and cook until crispy, about 5 minutes. Remove the bacon to a plate and set aside.

Add the pork shoulder to the same pot and sear until browned on all sides, 8 to 10 minutes. Remove the pork shoulder from the pot to a plate, add the onions and garlic to the pot, and cook until softened, 4 to 6 minutes. Add the sauerkraut, juniper, caraway, bay leaves, black pepper, and a large pinch of salt. Deglaze the pot with the wine and reduce it until it is almost fully absorbed. Add the chicken stock, pork shoulder, and bacon. Cover the cocotte, place it in the oven, and braise for 2 hours. Add the potatoes and cook for 1 hour more, or until the potatoes are softened and the pork shoulder is fork-tender. Remove the pork shoulder from the pot, leaving the oven on. Cool slightly, then shred the pork shoulder using your hands or two forks and return the meat to the pot.

While the pork shoulder is cooling, in a medium cast-iron fry pan, sear the sausages over medium-high heat until lightly browned, 4 to 6 minutes. Add the sausages to the cocotte, cover, return to the oven, and roast for an additional 15 to 20 minutes, until the sausages are warmed through. Remove from the oven and serve with the mustards and warm marbled rye bread.

CONFIT LAMB WITH RHUBARB MOSTARDA AND HORSERADISH GREMOLATA FROM ANGIE MAR OF THE BEATRICE INN

MAKES 8 TO 10 SERVINGS

LAMB CONFIT

4 bone-in lamb shanks (about 1½ pounds each)

¼ teaspoon kosher salt, plus more for seasoning the lamb

1 cup cloves garlic, peeled

1 tablespoon chopped fresh rosemary

4 tablespoons olive oil

About 2 quarts canola oil

RHUBARB MOSTARDA

8 stalks rhubarb, thinly sliced

¼ cup white wine

¼ cup white wine vinegar

½ cup sugar, or to taste

2 whole cloves

3 sprigs thyme

Salt and freshly ground black pepper

1½ tablespoons Dijon mustard

HORSERADISH GREMOLATA

3 tablespoons grated horseradish

2 tablespoons finely chopped fresh flat-leaf parsley

2 tablespoons finely chopped fresh mint

Zest of 2 lemons

This recipe is emblematic of New York City chef Angie Mar's talents, with succulent lamb shanks slathered in two Italian condiments: sweet mostarda and bright gremolata.

Make the lamb confit: Preheat the oven to 250°F. Season the lamb shanks liberally with salt. Place on a baking sheet and let sit in the refrigerator while you make the garlic paste.

In a food processor, combine the garlic cloves, rosemary, and ¼ teaspoon salt. With the machine running, slowly add 2 tablespoons olive oil. Coat the lamb shanks with the garlic paste. Place the the marinated shanks in an extra-large cast-iron cocotte and cover completely in canola oil. Cover with aluminum foil, place in the oven, and roast until the lamb is fragrant, tender, and almost falling off the bone, 2½ to 3 hours. Remove from the oven and set aside until you are ready to serve.

Make the rhubarb mostarda: In a petite French oven, combine the rhubarb, wine, vinegar, sugar, cloves, and thyme and bring to a boil over medium-high heat. Reduce the heat to low and simmer for 10 to 15 minutes, until syrupy. Season with salt and pepper and carefully remove the cloves and thyme. Turn off the heat and stir in the mustard. Set aside.

Make the horseradish gremolata: In a small bowl, combine the grated horseradish, parsley, mint, and lemon zest. Set aside until ready to serve.

When ready to serve, preheat the oven to 350°F. Remove the lamb shanks from the oil. Heat a 12-inch cast-iron fry pan with the remaining 2 tablespoons olive oil over medium-high heat. Add the lamb shanks and sear on all sides until they are a golden-brown color all over, 8 to 10 minutes. Place the shanks in a large cast-iron roasting pan and place it in the oven to heat through, 8 to 10 minutes.

Transfer the lamb shanks to a serving platter. Spoon the warm rhubarb mostarda over the shanks, sprinkle with the gremolata, and serve.

BLACK PEPPER AND PORCINI-CRUSTED FILET WITH HERBED BUTTER

½ cup unsalted butter, at room temperature

2 tablespoons chopped fresh chives

2 tablespoons chopped fresh rosemary

1 clove garlic, minced

Salt and freshly ground black pepper

½ ounce dried porcini mushrooms

2 tablespoons vegetable oil

4 (6-ounce) filet mignon steaks (1½ inches thick)

Herbed butter is a steak's best friend. With this classic French accompaniment, the butter melts into the meat for added juiciness, while its herbs help mellow the meat's fat. Steak is actually one of the easiest foods to cook in cast iron. The cast iron retains heat so well that you are guaranteed to get a nice sear. But when you're cooking indoors, it can get smoky, so this recipe calls for finishing the steak in the oven. If you have a large fry pan that can fit all four steaks, great. Don't worry if you don't have one—just cook the steaks in batches to prevent overcrowding the pan.

Preheat the oven to 425°F.

In a small bowl, combine the butter, chives, rosemary, garlic, and a pinch each of salt and pepper. Mix well and set aside.

In a spice grinder or blender, finely grind the dried porcinis, then pour them onto a plate in an even layer. Liberally sprinkle the steaks with salt and pepper, then press the steaks into the porcini powder.

Pour the oil into a large cast-iron fry pan and heat it over medium-high heat until barely smoking. Sear the steaks for 3 minutes per side, then place the pan in the oven for about 3 minutes, until the internal temperature reads 125°F on a meat thermometer for medium rare. Remove the steaks from the oven and place them on a plate. Cover with aluminum foil and let the steaks rest for 5 minutes, then top with a dollop of the herbed butter and serve.

GRILLED BONE-IN RIB EYE TOPPED WITH SHALLOT COMPOTE AND WATERCRESS

FROM CHEF BERNARD JANSSEN OF STAUB

MAKES 2 TO 4 SERVINGS

COMPOTE

2 tablespoons butter

10 shallots, diced

1 clove garlic, thinly sliced

3 sprigs thyme

¼ cup sherry vinegar

½ cup red wine

Salt and freshly ground black pepper

RIB EYE

Salt and freshly ground black pepper

2 (1 pound) bone-in rib eye steaks (1 to 1½ inches thick) at room temperature

WATERCRESS SALAD

3 tablespoons olive oil

1 tablespoon lemon juice

½ teaspoon balsamic vinegar

Kosher salt and freshly ground black pepper

3 cups packed watercress

The key to successful steaks is not only cooking them correctly but also seasoning them correctly. You can salt and pepper your steaks a couple hours beforehand, then place them uncovered in the refrigerator. As the salt and pepper work their way into the meat's muscles, the seasoning will penetrate beyond the outer surface for flavor throughout. This also enables you to get a better sear, as does this butter-basting method that creates a rich brown crust. Let the meat come to room temperature before cooking, which will allow for more even cooking. And resist the urge to flip your steaks until they release and are completely seared on the underside.

Make the compote: Melt the butter in a petite French oven. Add the shallots, garlic, and thyme, and cook for about 2 minutes, or until the shallots are translucent. Add the sherry vinegar, red wine, and pinch each of salt and pepper, and cook over low for 30 to 35 minutes, or until the compote has reduced and the shallots are very soft. Remove from heat and set aside.

Cook the steaks: Preheat a cast-iron grill pan over medium-high heat. Sprinkle the rib eyes liberally with salt and pepper. Place the rib eyes on the grill pan and cook for 7 minutes. Flip the steaks and cook for another 3 to 5 minutes for medium rare, until the internal temperature is 125°F. Remove the steaks from the grill pan and let rest for at least 5 minutes.

While the steaks rest, make the watercress salad: In a medium bowl, whisk together the olive oil, lemon juice, balsamic vinegar, and pinch each of salt and pepper. Add the watercress and toss well to cover the leaves.

Slice the steaks and top immediately with a dollop of compote and a handful of watercress.

DESSERTS

Strawberry Crumble
with Oats and Hazelnuts 177

Apricot Almond Yogurt Cake 178

Peach Cobbler
with Shortcake Crust 181

Pineapple Upside-Down
Griddle Cake 182

Vanilla Bean and Sage
Blackberry Galette 185

Cherry Clafoutis with Crème
Fraîche Whipped Cream 186

Plantia's Tarte Tatin 189

Maple-Spiced Anjou
Pear Crumble 190

Gingerbread Cake with Cinnamon
Cream Cheese Frosting 191

Pecan Butterscotch
Bread Pudding 192

Toffee Blondie 195

Grilled Brown Sugar Bourbon
Pound Cake with Ice Cream
and Berries 196

Brûléed Rice Pudding
with Apricots 199

Pumpkin Pots de Crème 200

Spiced Chocolate Fondue 202

Chocolate Soufflé with
Mint Crème Anglaise 205

Flourless Chocolate
Orange Cakes 209

STRAWBERRY CRUMBLE WITH OATS AND HAZELNUTS

MAKES 6 TO 8 SERVINGS

CRUMBLE TOPPING

1 cup old-fashioned rolled oats

1½ cups all-purpose flour

¾ cup brown sugar

1 cup unsalted butter, cut into cubes

¾ cup chopped hazelnuts

Pinch of salt

¼ teaspoon freshly grated nutmeg

STRAWBERRY FILLING

3 pounds strawberries

½ cup lightly packed light brown sugar

3 tablespoons cornstarch

1 tablespoon fresh lemon juice

1 tablespoon lemon zest

Pinch of salt

Packed with farm-fresh strawberries, this crumble is the perfect way to sweeten a summertime barbecue. Oats and hazelnuts add heft to the buttery brown-sugar crumble topping. Feel free to use other fruits such as blueberries, cherries, or raspberries for your crumble. The ample topping absorbs all the delicious liquid from the fruit, creating a perfect crunchy-soft texture. The cast-iron fry pan doubles as as homespun serving dish. Just don't forget the ice cream or whipped cream!

Preheat the oven to 375°F.

Make the crumble topping: In the bowl of a stand mixer fitted with the paddle attachment, combine the oats, flour, brown sugar, butter, hazelnuts, salt, and nutmeg. Mix on low speed until the mixture comes together in small clumps. Set aside.

Make the strawberry filling: In a large bowl, combine the strawberries, light brown sugar, cornstarch, lemon juice, lemon zest, and salt. Let the berries macerate on the counter for about 10 minutes, then place them in a medium cast-iron fry pan.

Crumble the topping over the strawberry filling in the pan and bake for 55 minutes to 1 hour, until the filling is bubbling and the crust is golden brown. Remove from the oven and let cool for at least 20 minutes before serving.

APRICOT ALMOND YOGURT CAKE

FROM ATHENA CALDERONE OF EYESWOON

5 ripe but firm apricots

1 cup all-purpose flour

¾ cup almond meal

1 teaspoon baking powder

¾ teaspoon kosher salt

1 teaspoon fresh thyme leaves, plus more for sprinkling (optional)

1 cup unsalted butter, at room temperature

¾ cup granulated sugar

2 large eggs

½ cup full-fat plain Greek yogurt

1 tablespoon bourbon

3 tablespoons raw demerara sugar

FOR SERVING

Whipped cream

Athena Calderone, who runs the gorgeous food and lifestyle blog *Eyeswoon*, has flawlessly demonstrated how yogurt can elevate a baked good. Yogurt makes the cake marvelously moist, its flavor subtly sweet from bourbon and demerara sugar. Savory thyme plays nicely with the apricots.

Preheat the oven to 350°F.

Butter a medium cast-iron fry pan and nestle a piece of parchment into the pan so the parchment is hanging over on all sides. Slice the apricots in half lengthwise and remove the pits. Slice one apricot into ¼-inch half-moon slices and reserve for topping the cake. Cut the remaining apricots into ¾-inch cubes. Set aside.

Sift into a large bowl the flour, almond meal, baking powder, and salt and add the thyme.

Combine the butter and granulated sugar in the bowl of a stand mixer and beat until light and fluffy, about 4 minutes. Add the eggs, one at a time, making sure each is fully incorporated before adding the next. Beat until the mixture is pale and fluffy, about 4 minutes. Scrape down the sides, reduce the speed to low, and gradually add the dry ingredients. Add the yogurt and bourbon and stir until just combined. Using a spatula, fold in the chopped apricots, then scrape the batter into the prepared pan. Smooth the batter and arrange the reserved apricot slices on top in a cylindrical pattern, overlapping slightly.

Sprinkle with demerara sugar and bake for 50 to 55 minutes, rotating the pan once, until a toothpick inserted into the center of the cake comes out clean. Transfer to a wire rack and cool completely. Serve with a dollop of whipped cream and sprinkle with thyme leaves.

PEACH COBBLER WITH SHORTCAKE CRUST

FROM MARK WELKER OF ELEVEN MADISON PARK

MAKE 6 TO 8 SERVINGS

SHORTCAKE

1¼ cups all-purpose flour

¼ cup granulated sugar

1 tablespoon baking powder

½ teaspoon salt

1 teaspoon lemon zest

Seeds from 1 vanilla bean or
1 tablespoon vanilla extract

½ cup cold unsalted
butter, diced

¼ cup cold heavy cream

PEACH FILLING

Softened butter, for greasing

⅓ cup plus 1 tablespoon
all-purpose flour, plus more
for rolling

¼ cup granulated sugar

1¾ pounds peaches, chopped

1 teaspoon lemon zest

¼ cup orange juice

1 tablespoon fresh lemon
juice

2 tablespoons cold unsalted
butter, diced

Melted butter and turbinado
sugar, for topping

FOR SERVING

Vanilla ice cream

Peach cobbler is the ultimate summertime dessert. While this old-fashioned dessert can be made with any batter or biscuit, here a buttery shortcake ups this cobbler's appeal. Chef Mark Welker mixes the peaches with citrus to bring out the best of the stone fruit. Make sure to serve this delicious version with a large scoop of vanilla ice cream.

Make the shortcake: In a large bowl, combine the flour, granulated sugar, baking powder, salt, lemon zest, vanilla seeds, and butter. Using your hands, press the butter into the flour until the mixture resembles coarse cornmeal. Add the cream and mix until a dough forms. Knead the dough a few times, adding a small amount of flour if the dough is too wet. Wrap the dough in plastic wrap and let rest for 30 minutes in the refrigerator.

While the dough is resting, make the peach filling: Preheat the oven to 350°F. Rub a medium oval cast-iron roasting or fry pan with softened butter.

In a medium bowl, whisk the flour with the granulated sugar. Set aside.

In a large bowl, mix the peaches with the lemon zest, then add the flour-sugar mixture and toss to coat the peaches. Add the orange juice and lemon juice. Stir until the peaches are well coated. Add the filling to the prepared pan and scatter the cold butter on top.

On a well-floured surface, roll the shortcake out into a large oval or round about ⅛ inch thick. Cover the filling with the shortcake, brush with melted butter, and sprinkle with turbinado sugar. Bake until the crust is golden brown and the filling is bubbling, 50 to 60 minutes. Let cool for 30 minutes before scooping, and serve with vanilla ice cream.

PINEAPPLE UPSIDE-DOWN GRIDDLE CAKE

FROM DAVID LEFEVRE OF MANHATTAN BEACH POST, FISHING WITH DYNAMITE, AND THE ARTHUR J

MAKES 6 TO 8 SERVINGS

CAKE

2 tablespoons clarified butter

5 fresh pineapple rings

3 cups all-purpose flour

I cup semolina flour

2¼ tablespoons sugar

2 tablespoons baking powder

2 teaspoons baking soda

Pinch of salt

4 large eggs

I cup sour cream

1¾ cups milk

¾ cup vegetable oil

I teaspoon vanilla extract

½ vanilla bean, cut in half and seeds scraped out

Zest of I lemon

MARASCHINO CHERRY BUTTER

I cup unsalted butter, at room temperature

¼ cup maraschino cherries

2 tablespoons maraschino cherry juice

FOR SERVING

Maple syrup

There's nothing more comforting than a moist pineapple upside-down cake. Chef David LeFevre, of Southern California's Manhattan Beach Post, adds a twist to the iconic American dessert with a marvelous maraschino cherry butter that ups the brown-butter flavor. It contains very little sugar, but a drizzle of maple at the table provides a sweet finish.

Preheat the oven to 375°F.

Make the cake: In a medium cast-iron fry pan, heat the butter over medium-low heat. Add the pineapple and cook until softened and golden brown, flipping once, 4 to 6 minutes. Remove the fry pan from the heat.

In a large bowl, combine the flours, sugar, baking powder, baking soda, and salt. Set aside.

In the bowl of a stand mixer, combine the eggs, sour cream, milk, vegetable oil, vanilla extract, vanilla bean seeds, and lemon zest. Mix on low speed until combined. Slowly add the dry ingredients until completely incorporated.

Pour the batter over the pineapple rings and bake for 35 to 40 minutes, until a toothpick inserted in the cake comes out clean.

While the cake is baking, make the maraschino cherry butter: Clean out the bowl of the stand mixer, add the butter, maraschino cherries, and cherry juice and mix until combined. Let cool in the refrigerator while the cake bakes.

Carefully flip the cake onto a plate. Slice, top with the maraschino cherry butter, and serve with a drizzle of maple syrup.

VANILLA BEAN AND SAGE BLACKBERRY GALETTE

FROM LILY DIAMOND OF *KALE & CARAMEL*

CRUST

1¼ cups all-purpose flour

2 tablespoons sugar

1 tablespoon finely chopped fresh sage

½ teaspoon kosher salt

½ cup chilled unsalted butter, cut into cubes

¼ cup sour cream

¼ teaspoon vanilla bean paste

BLACKBERRY SAGE FILLING

18 ounces fresh blackberries

3 tablespoons sugar, plus more for sprinkling

1 tablespoon cornstarch

2 teaspoons finely chopped fresh sage

Pinch of sea salt

1 teaspoon fresh lemon juice

¼ teaspoon vanilla bean paste

1 large egg, beaten

Lily Diamond, of the blog and eponymous cookbook *Kale & Caramel*, has the unique ability to weave herbs and flowers into her cooking, creating delicious masterpieces. In this galette, she adds vanilla bean and sage to complement blackberries in the best possible way.

Make the crust: In a large bowl, whisk together the flour, sugar, sage, and kosher salt. Add the butter and use a fork or pastry cutter to blend in the butter until it is in pea-size bits. Add the sour cream and vanilla bean paste and continue to blend just until the dough comes together smoothly. Shape into a ½-inch disk, cover with plastic wrap, and refrigerate for at least 1 hour or up to 2 days.

While the dough is chilling, make the filling: In a large bowl, combine the blackberries, sugar, cornstarch, sage, sea salt, lemon juice, and vanilla bean paste. Toss lightly to mix the ingredients and coat the berries evenly.

Preheat the oven to 400°F and lightly butter a medium cast-iron fry pan.

Place a piece of parchment paper on a clean, dry surface for rolling and sprinkle it with flour. Place the chilled dough on the parchment paper and sprinkle with a bit more flour. Roll the dough out to a 12-inch circle that's about ¼ inch thick. Use the parchment paper to flip the dough into the fry pan, laying it out evenly in the base and sides of the pan.

Place the berry mixture in the center of the dough and spread it out, leaving a 2- to 2½-inch border of dough. Fold the exposed dough over the berries in pleats, pressing the dough together to seal completely. Brush the beaten egg over the exposed dough and sprinkle with sugar.

Bake for 35 to 40 minutes, until the crust is deep golden in color and the berries are bubbling. Remove from the oven and cool for at least 30 minutes before serving.

CHERRY CLAFOUTIS WITH CRÈME FRAÎCHE WHIPPED CREAM

MAKES 6 TO 8 SERVINGS

CLAFOUTIS

1¼ pounds fresh cherries, pitted

4 large eggs

½ cup brown sugar

½ cup all-purpose flour

2 teaspoons vanilla extract

1 tablespoon kirsch liqueur

1¼ cups half-and-half

½ teaspoon salt

Turbinado sugar

WHIPPED CREAM

1 cup heavy cream

¼ cup crème fraîche

2 tablespoons granulated sugar

Powdered sugar, for garnish

One look at clafoutis and you might imagine this sophisticated French dessert would include lots of steps and complicated directions. In reality, it couldn't be easier; it is simply a straightforward custard speckled with fruit. To make this recipe, a crepe-like batter is poured around cherries and baked until set. The traditional clafoutis is made with cherries, but other stone fruit, like sliced apricots and Italian plums, would also work. If you can't find kirsch—a cherry-flavored liquor—swap in ½ teaspoon almond extract.

Make the clafoutis: Preheat the oven to 375°F. Butter an 8 by 5½-inch oval cast-iron roasting pan.

Arrange the cherries in the prepared pan in a single layer. Set aside.

In a blender, combine the eggs, brown sugar, flour, vanilla, kirsch, half-and-half, and salt. Blend on high speed for about 30 seconds, until well blended. Pour the mixture over the cherries and add a sprinkle of turbinado sugar. Bake for 40 to 50 minutes, until the custard is set and lightly browned.

While the clafoutis is baking, make the whipped cream: In the bowl of a stand mixer, combine the cream, crème fraîche, and granulated sugar, and beat until soft peaks form.

Serve the clafoutis with a sprinkle of powdered sugar and a dollop of the whipped cream.

PLANTIA'S TARTE TATIN

FROM MIMI THORISSON OF MANGER

DOUGH

1½ cups all-purpose flour, sifted, plus more for rolling

⅓ cup sugar

Pinch of fine sea salt

1 large egg yolk

7 tablespoons cold unsalted butter, cut into small pieces

APPLES

½ cup sugar

1 vanilla bean, split lengthwise, seeds scraped

6½ tablespoons unsalted butter, cut into small pieces

2½ pounds apples, peeled, cored, and quartered

FOR SERVING

Crème fraîche

Mimi Thorisson's popular blog, *Manger*, reads like a fantasy set in the French countryside. This tarte tatin recipe is her ode to the previous owner of her house in Médoc and is adapted from her cookbook *French Country Cooking*. Tarte tatin is a delightful dessert to make in the fall when apples are at their prime.

Make the dough: Place the flour in a large bowl and make a well in the center. Add the sugar, salt, and egg yolk, and mix slowly with your hands. Add the butter and mix until you have a smooth and homogenous dough. Form the dough into a ball, cover with plastic wrap, and refrigerate for at least 1 hour or overnight.

Preheat the oven to 350°F. Butter a 10-inch cast-iron fry pan.

Prepare the apples: In a medium bowl, mix the sugar with the vanilla bean seeds. Sprinkle the vanilla sugar over the bottom of the fry pan, scatter the butter over the sugar, then tightly pack the apples in the pan in a circular fashion, with one flat side down.

Set the fry pan over medium-high heat and cook until the apple liquid starts to bubble, about 3 minutes. Reduce the heat and continue to cook until the juices turn a golden caramel color, about 10 minutes. Remove from the heat.

On a lightly floured work surface, roll out the dough ⅛ inch thick. Using a sharp knife, cut a round of dough just slightly larger than the top of the fry pan. Drape the dough over the apples to cover them and carefully use your fingers to tuck the dough between the pan and the apples all around. Transfer to the oven and bake until the pastry is golden brown, about 40 minutes.

Remove from the oven and let cool for 5 minutes. Carefully unmold the tatin by placing a large serving plate on top of the pan and inverting the cake onto the plate. Serve with crème fraîche.

MAPLE-SPICED ANJOU PEAR CRUMBLE

FROM DAVID LEE OF NOTA BENE

MAKES 6 TO 8 SERVINGS

CRUMBLE TOPPING

½ cup brown sugar

½ cup granulated sugar

Pinch of salt

14 tablespoons unsalted butter, melted and cooled

2 cups all-purpose flour

PEAR FILLING

½ cup maple syrup

2 tablespoons fresh lemon juice

Pinch of salt

2 tablespoons all-purpose flour

2½ pounds Anjou pears (about 5), peeled, cored, and cut into 2-inch wedges

½ cup packed sultana raisins

Everything about chef David Lee's spiced pears screams fall. Owner of Toronto's Nota Bene, Lee sweetens the pears with maple syrup, and a brown sugar crumble ties the dish together. It's a very easy recipe to assemble, especially if you make the crumble in advance, meaning there is no excuse for not having homemade dessert.

Preheat the oven to 350°F.

Make the crumble topping: In a large bowl, combine the sugars and salt. Add the melted butter and flour and stir until walnut-size pieces are formed. Set aside.

Make the pear filling: In a large bowl, whisk the maple syrup, lemon juice, salt, and flour. Fold in the pears and raisins.

Transfer the pear mixture to a medium cast-iron roasting pan or fry pan. Top the pears with the crumble topping and bake for 40 to 50 minutes, until the crumble is golden brown. Let cool for 10 minutes, then serve warm.

GINGERBREAD CAKE WITH CINNAMON CREAM CHEESE FROSTING

CAKE

2⅓ cups all-purpose flour

I teaspoon baking soda

2 teaspoons ground ginger

2 teaspoons ground cinnamon

½ teaspoon ground cloves

½ teaspoon salt

½ cup unsalted butter,
at room temperature

⅓ cup brown sugar

I cup molasses

¾ cup hot water

2 large eggs

FROSTING

½ cup unsalted butter

2 cups powdered sugar

2 tablespoons heavy cream

I teaspoon vanilla extract

I teaspoon ground cinnamon

Pinch of salt

8 ounces cream cheese,
at room temperature

This recipe was inspired by a cake made by the wife of Staub's head of sales. It was such a hit at a Staub retreat that it quickly became a company-wide favorite, thanks to its rich molasses, brown sugar, and the warming spices that make fall desserts so comforting.

Make the cake: Preheat the oven to 325°F. Butter an 8 by 12-inch rectangular cast-iron roasting pan.

In a medium bowl, whisk together the flour, baking soda, ginger, cinnamon, cloves, and salt. Set aside. In the bowl of a stand mixer, cream the butter and brown sugar. Mix in the molasses and hot water. Let cool slightly, then beat in the eggs. Add the dry ingredients and beat until just combined.

Pour the cake batter into prepared pan and bake for 45 to 50 minutes, until a toothpick barely comes out clean. Let the cake cool.

Make the frosting: In the bowl of a stand mixer, mix the butter with the powdered sugar, cream, vanilla, cinnamon, and salt. Add the cream cheese and mix until smooth. Refrigerate until you are ready to frost the cake.

Just before serving, frost the cake and cut it into squares.

PECAN BUTTERSCOTCH BREAD PUDDING

MAKES 6 TO 8 SERVINGS

BREAD PUDDING

6 large eggs

3 cups heavy cream

I cup granulated sugar

I teaspoon vanilla extract

Pinch of salt

I (I-pound) day-old rustic white bread, such as ciabatta, crusts removed, cut into I-inch cubes

I cup toasted pecan pieces

BUTTERSCOTCH

½ cup unsalted butter

I cup packed light brown sugar

I½ teaspoons salt

I cup heavy cream

I tablespoon vanilla extract

FOR SERVING

Vanilla ice cream

Unfussy desserts are always winners, and bread pudding tops the list. A good bread pudding starts with stale, dry bread to soak up the creamy, eggy goodness. This recipe adds pecans and butterscotch for Southern flair. If you make the butterscotch in advance, be careful when rewarming it, as it has a tendency to break when it's reheated too fast. If it does break, whisk in a couple tablespoons of heavy cream until it's smooth and silky again.

Make the bread pudding: Butter a 10 by 15-inch rectangular cast-iron roasting pan.

In a large bowl, whisk together the eggs, cream, granulated sugar, vanilla, and salt. Add the bread and toss well. Fold in the pecans and toss well to coat. Pour the mixture into the prepared pan, cover with plastic wrap, and refrigerate overnight.

Remove the pan from the refrigerator and preheat the oven to 350°F.

Cover the pan with aluminum foil and bake for 1 hour. Remove the foil and bake for another 15 to 20 minutes, until the top is golden brown. Remove from the oven and let cool slightly.

Make the butterscotch: In a petite French oven, melt the butter over medium heat. Add the brown sugar, salt, and cream and whisk until smooth. Bring to a boil and cook for about 5 minutes, until a thick and syrupy butterscotch is formed. Add the vanilla, stir, and set aside until ready to serve.

Serve the bread pudding with a drizzle of butterscotch and a scoop of vanilla ice cream.

TOFFEE BLONDIE

2¼ cups all-purpose flour

1½ teaspoons baking soda

¼ teaspoon salt

1 cup unsalted butter, at room temperature

1¼ cups brown sugar

2 large eggs

1 large egg yolk

1 tablespoon vanilla extract

4½ ounces chocolate-covered toffee, such as a Heath bar, chopped

FOR SERVING

Vanilla ice cream

Part brownie, part cookie, and fully delicious, this giant blondie gets a sweet, buttery crunch from toffee bits. If you can't find prepared toffee in the candy aisle at the grocery store, feel free to use chocolate chips instead. For a gooey center, pull the blondie from the oven after about 35 minutes, when the edges are crispy and the center isn't quite set. For a firmer center, keep it in the oven for another 5 to 10 minutes. Serve the blondie still warm and in the fry pan, with a bunch of spoons and ice cream, of course.

Preheat the oven to 350°F. Butter a 10-inch cast-iron fry pan.

In a medium bowl, whisk together the flour, baking soda, and salt. Set aside.

In the bowl of a stand mixer, cream the butter and brown sugar until light and creamy. Add the eggs, egg yolk, and vanilla and mix until well combined. Add the flour mixture to the butter mixture and mix until just combined. Fold in the toffee, pour the batter into the prepared pan, and smooth into an even layer. Bake for 30 to 40 minutes, depending on how gooey you want the middle of the blondie to be. Let it cool for 10 minutes before serving warm with scoops of vanilla ice cream.

GRILLED BROWN SUGAR BOURBON POUND CAKE WITH ICE CREAM AND BERRIES

MAKES 6 TO 8 SERVINGS

1½ cups all-purpose flour

1 teaspoon baking powder

Pinch of salt

½ cup unsalted butter, at room temperature, plus more for brushing

1 cup brown sugar

2 large eggs

½ cup whole milk

1 tablespoon bourbon

½ teaspoon almond extract

FOR SERVING

Vanilla ice cream and fresh berries

This is an updated take on that nostalgic childhood treat, ice cream cake. The pound cake comes together really easily, and by grilling it, a whole new crispy, smoky component is added. If you don't have bourbon, you could substitute dark rum or vanilla extract. Sweet berries pair wonderfully with the bourbon notes in the pound cake, but any seasonal fresh fruit will work. When you add the milk to the butter mixture, it may look broken. Not to worry, it's just the butter seizing up from the cold milk; it will smooth out once the flour is added.

Preheat the oven to 325°F. Coat a 9 by 5-inch cast-iron loaf pan with butter or oil.

In a small bowl, combine the flour, baking powder, and salt. Set aside.

In the bowl of a stand mixer, cream the butter and brown sugar. Add the eggs one at a time, followed by the milk, bourbon, and almond extract. Fold in the flour mixture. Pour the batter into the prepared pan and bake for 50 to 55 minutes, until a toothpick comes out clean. Remove from the pan and let cool completely.

Preheat a cast-iron grill pan over medium-low heat. Cut the pound cake into 1-inch slices and lightly brush with butter. Grill the slices for 3 to 4 minutes per side, until golden brown and grill marks appear. Top the warm pound cake with a scoop of ice cream and fresh berries and serve immediately.

BRÛLÉED RICE PUDDING WITH APRICOTS

FROM VALERIE GORDON OF VALERIE CONFECTIONS

MAKES 4 TO 6 SERVINGS

2 teaspoons unsalted butter

½ cup short-grain rice

½ teaspoon kosher salt

1 teaspoon vanilla bean paste

1 teaspoon ground cardamom

4 cups whole milk, at room temperature

½ cup dried apricots, diced

½ cup packed light brown sugar

¼ cup granulated sugar

As a busy mom and small business owner, Los Angeles chocolatier and baker Valerie Gordon appreciates an uncomplicated dessert. Rice pudding is a great make-ahead recipe, plus the basic ingredients are pantry staples. Gordon gives elegance to the homey pudding by adding fragrant cardamom and dried apricots and deliciously browning the crust crème brûlée–style. This is a great dessert to serve to guests, as you can make it the day before and keep it chilled in the refrigerator. Simply add sugar to the top and torch before serving.

Melt the butter in a small oval cast-iron roasting dish on the stovetop over medium-low heat.

Stir in the rice, salt, vanilla bean paste, and cardamom, and continue cooking until the rice is golden and coated with the spices and butter.

Increase the heat to medium and stream in the milk in ½-cup increments, allowing the rice to absorb about half of the milk with each addition. Add the apricots and brown sugar and continue cooking until the rice is expanded and cooked through, 10 to 15 minutes.

Remove from the heat and cover the surface tightly with plastic wrap. Cool to room temperature, then chill in the refrigerator for at least 2 hours, until cold.

When you are ready to serve, sprinkle the granulated sugar over the pudding and brûlée either with a kitchen torch or under the broiler set to high. Serve immediately.

PUMPKIN POTS DE CRÈME

MAKES 6 SERVINGS

POTS DE CRÈME

2 cups half-and-half

½ cup packed light brown sugar

I cup canned solid-pack pumpkin (not pumpkin pie puree)

6 large egg yolks

I teaspoon ground cinnamon

Pinch of ground cloves

Pinch of freshly grated nutmeg

Pinch of salt

WHIPPED TOPPING

I cup heavy cream

3 tablespoons maple syrup

3 amaretti cookies, crumbled

Filled with warming spices, these pots de crème are a pretty way to ring in fall and the holiday season. Baked in adorable individually-sized cocottes, they save you the hassle of making a pie. Don't worry crust-lovers—these pots de crème are sprinkled with amaretti, Italian almond cookies, for a toothsome crunch. If you are able, make these the day before serving them so there is time for the flavors to mingle.

Make the pots de crème: Preheat the oven to 325°F.

In a petite French oven, whisk the half-and-half, ¼ cup of the brown sugar, and the pumpkin. Bring to a simmer over medium heat, then remove from the heat and keep warm.

In a medium bowl, whisk together the egg yolks, the remaining ¼ cup brown sugar, the cinnamon, cloves, nutmeg, and salt. Slowly pour in the half-and-half mixture, whisking constantly. Divide the mixture among 6 mini cast-iron cocottes. Place the cocottes in a large cast-iron roasting pan and carefully fill with water to come halfway up the sides of the cocottes.

Bake until the custard is just barely set in the middle, 45 to 50 minutes. Remove the pan from the oven and remove the cocottes from the roasting pan. Allow to cool to room temperature. Cover and place in the refrigerator for at least 3 hours, until fully chilled.

Make the whipped topping: In the bowl of a stand mixer, combine the cream and maple syrup and whip until soft peaks form. Top each cocotte with a dollop of whipped cream and some amaretti cookie crumbles to serve.

SPICED CHOCOLATE FONDUE

MAKES 4 SERVINGS

1 cup heavy cream

1 cinnamon stick,
broken in half

2 cardamom pods,
lightly crushed

2 whole cloves

Pinch of freshly grated
nutmeg

Pinch of ground cayenne

Pinch of flaky sea salt

8 ounces semisweet
chocolate, chopped

FOR SERVING

Fruit

Grilled Brown Sugar
Bourbon Pound Cake
(optional, page 196)

Vanilla Bean Old-Fashioned
Doughnuts (optional, page 23)

The chocolate in the fondue is flavored with warm spices like cinnamon and cardamom which brings just a hint of depth of flavor to the chocolate. Serve this spiced fondue with assorted fruit, Brown Sugar Bourbon Pound Cake, or, if you're feeling a little wild, Vanilla Bean Old-Fashioned Doughnuts.

In a cast-iron petite French oven, combine the cream, cinnamon, cardamom, cloves, nutmeg, and cayenne. Bring to a simmer, then remove from the heat. Let the spices steep into the cream for 20 minutes. Strain the cream, then return it to the French oven over medium-low heat, until the cream just barely simmers.

Place the chocolate in a medium heatproof bowl. Pour the hot cream over the chocolate and leave it for a few minutes to melt the chocolate. Whisk until smooth, then pour the mixture into a fondue pot. Serve the fondue with fruit, pound cake, or doughnuts for dipping.

CHOCOLATE SOUFFLÉ
WITH MINT CRÈME ANGLAISE

MINT CRÈME ANGLAISE

1 cup half-and-half

½ vanilla bean, split

1 cup fresh mint leaves

3 large egg yolks

¼ cup granulated sugar

SOUFFLÉ

½ cup granulated sugar, plus more for coating the pan

6 ounces bittersweet chocolate

½ cup heavy cream, warmed

2 teaspoons vanilla extract

Pinch of salt

4 large egg yolks

5 large egg whites

1 teaspoon cream of tartar

Powdered sugar, for sprinkling

Soufflés have a reputation for being difficult and finicky, but with a couple tips and techniques, they are in fact easy to master. The first important rule is to fold rather than stir in the egg whites; this helps keep them buoyant so you get that wonderful rise in the oven. The second rule is to butter and sugar the sides of the baking dish; this helps the soufflé to rise. Make sure to have the crème anglaise ready to go before you bake the soufflé, as soufflés are best devoured right out of the oven.

Make the mint crème anglaise: In a petite French oven, combine the half-and-half, vanilla bean, and mint. Bring just barely to a boil over medium heat, then pour into a bowl and cover with plastic wrap. Let the vanilla and mint infuse the cream for 20 minutes. Strain the cream and keep it warm.

In medium bowl, whisk the egg yolks and granulated sugar. Gradually whisk ¼ cup of the warm cream into the egg yolks. Slowly whisk in the remaining cream mixture. Return the cream to the French oven and cook over medium-low heat until the crème anglaise is thick enough to coat the back of a wooden spoon. Strain into a bowl, cover with plastic wrap, and chill until ready to serve.

Make the soufflé: Preheat the oven to 350°F. Butter a cast-iron petite French oven. Sprinkle the pot with sugar, coating the sides and bottom. Discard any extra sugar.

In a large bowl, combine the chocolate and warm cream. Let sit for 2 to 3 minutes, then whisk until smooth. Add ¼ cup of the granulated sugar,

continued

the vanilla extract, and salt and mix well. Add the egg yolks and whisk to combine. Set aside.

In the bowl of a stand mixer, combine the egg whites and cream of tartar and mix on low speed until small bubbles begin to form. Increase the speed to high and mix until soft peaks form. Sprinkle in the remaining ¼ cup granulated sugar, a small amount at a time, and continue to beat on high speed until smooth and glossy stiff peaks form.

Using a spatula, fold one-quarter of the egg white mixture into the chocolate mixture. Add the remaining egg whites, being careful not to overmix. Pour the mixture into the prepared French oven and bake for 23 to 27 minutes, until the soufflé has risen and the top appears set. Sprinkle with powdered sugar and serve immediately with the crème anglaise.

FLOURLESS CHOCOLATE ORANGE CAKES

I pound bittersweet chocolate, roughly chopped

I cup unsalted butter, cut into cubes

4 large eggs

I cup sugar

I teaspoon salt

I½ cup all-purpose flour

3 tablespoons orange zest, plus more for serving

2 tablespoon orange liqueur, such as Grand Marnier (optional)

FOR SERVING

Whipped cream

Mini cocottes are the ideal size for these intensely chocolatey cakes—you can enjoy them without overindulging. If you don't love the rich tartness of dark chocolate, you can substitute semisweet chocolate instead. This recipe spices up classic chocolate with orange zest and liqueur. Feel free to play around with other flavor combinations, such as peppermint extract, cinnamon, or candied ginger. You can find inspiration in the chocolate bars sold at your grocery store.

Preheat the oven to 350°F.

In a petite French oven, melt the chocolate with the butter over low heat, stirring until completely smooth. Let cool slightly.

In a medium bowl, whisk together the eggs, sugar, salt, flour, orange zest, and orange liqueur. Temper the egg mixture by slowly folding in ¼ cup of the warm chocolate mixture. Once incorporated, fold in the remaining chocolate and evenly divide the mixture among 6 mini cast-iron cocottes. Bake for 20 to 22 minutes, until the edges just begin to pull away from the sides of the pan and the center is barely set. Top with whipped cream and orange zest and serve immediately.

ACKNOWLEDGMENTS

To our author Amanda Frederickson, an enormous thank you for your partnership on this book. Your palate led us to great places, and we feel so fortunate to have found you. We can't wait to see what you cook up next. Thank you to Amanda's agent Berta Trietl, who was such a pleasure.

To our photo crew, we are eternally grateful for your vision, your attention to detail, and your enthusiasm for this project. Colin Price, photographer, Emily Caneer, stylist, Olivia Caminiti, stylist, and Glenn Jenkins, prop stylist: you made each recipe look as good as it tastes.

Our wordsmithing friends Amanda Sims and Alexis Steinman guided the tone throughout. And merci beaucoup to Devereaux Chatillon, who helped us navigate contracts and get to the fun part—the recipes!

This book was such a team effort and our dear friends at Ten Speed Press beautifully led the way. Hannah, Kelly, Windy, Emma, Lisa, Allison, Betsy, Daniel, Erin, and Jane, we couldn't have done this without your seasoned expertise and talents.

Finally, a special thanks to Meredith Bradford, who guided and cultivated this book from concept to print. Your endless commitment was a display in how it should be done!

Listed below are the contributors whose recipes made this book a reality. We're grateful to have you as part of our community.

Michelle Lopez, Hummingbird High

Tieghan Gerard, Half Baked Harvest

Jeanine Donofrio and Jack Mathews, Love and Lemons

Camille Styles, Camille Styles

Molly Yeh, My Name Is Yeh

Noah Goldberg, Peter Pan Bistro

Justin Devillier, La Petite Grocery

Stuart Cameron, Byblos and Patria

Nik Sharma, A Brown Table

Joseph Keller, The Company of the Cauldron

Erik Anderson, Coi

Dan Kluger, Loring Place

Paul Virant, Vie and Vistro

Julia Sullivan, Henrietta Red

Thea Bauman, co-author of It's All Easy

Matt Lewis and Renato Poliafito, Baked

Edward Lee, 610 Magnolia, Milkwood, Succotash, and Whisky Dry

Jonathan Waxman, Barbuto, JAMS, Brezza Cucina, and Adele's

Amanda Hesser and Merrill Stubbs, Food52

Christopher Kimball, Christopher Kimball's Milk Street

Alana Kysar, Fix Feast Flair

Stephanie Le, I Am a Food Blog

Marcus Ware, Greydon House

Julia Turshen, author of Small Victories, Feed the Resistance, and Now & Again

Floyd Cardoz, Bombay Bread Bar

Sean Pharr, Mint Mark

Angie Mar, The Beatrice Inn

Bernard Janssen, Staub

Athena Calderone, EyeSwoon

Mark Welker, Eleven Madison Park

David LeFevre, Manhattan Beach Post, Fishing with Dynamite, and The Arthur J

Lily Diamond, Kale & Caramel

Mimi Thorisson, Manger

David Lee, Nota Bene

Valerie Gordon, Valerie Confections

INDEX

Published in the United States by Ten Speed Press, an imprint of the Crown
Publishing Group, a division of Penguin Random House LLC, New York.
www.crownpublishing.com
www.tenspeed.com

Ten Speed Press and the Ten Speed Press colophon are registered trademarks
of Penguin Random House LLC.

Library of Congress Cataloging-in-Publication Data
Names: Frederickson, Amanda, author. | Price, Colin, (Photographer),
photographer. | Staub (Firm)
Title: The Staub cookbook : modern recipes for classic cast iron / by Staub
with Amanda Frederickson ; photography by Colin Price.
Description: California : Ten Speed Press, [2018] | Includes index.
Identifiers: LCCN 2018003401| ISBN 9780399580826 (hardcover) | ISBN
9780399580833 (ebook)
Subjects: LCSH: Dutch oven cooking. | Cast-iron. | LCGFT: Cookbooks.
Classification: LCC TX840.S55 F74 2018 | DDC 641.5/89--dc23
LC record available at https://lccn.loc.gov/2018003401

Hardcover ISBN: 978-0-399-58082-6
eBook ISBN: 978-0-399-58083-3

Printed in China

Design by Lisa Ferkel
Food styling by Emily Caneer with Olivia Caminiti
Prop styling by Glenn Jenkins

10 9 8 7 6 5 4 3 2 1

First Edition